HO

Wedding
coordinator

EVERYTHING YOU NEED TO KNOW
ABOUT WEDDING DAY MANAGEMENT

ALLISON FOSTER

HOW TO BE A WEDDING COORDINATOR

Copyright © 2020 by Allison Foster

Cover Design by Allison Foster and Kerry Watson

Book Formatting by Derek Murphy of Creativeindie Design

Author Photo by Jon Lundstrom of Junebug Photography

ISBN: 9798608785283

Contents

Introduction

So you're interested in becoming a wedding coordinator! Or perhaps you aspire to be a wedding *planner* and are looking for a place to start. Well give yourself a high-five because you have just taken your first step towards making that dream a reality! Wedding coordination is both an incredibly exciting and highly rewarding career. You get to help couples fully enjoy the best day of their lives! What could be better than that?

In writing this book, my goal was to eliminate all of the guesswork for someone who is just beginning their career as a wedding coordinator. Starting out in the wedding industry can feel incredibly overwhelming! You can know everything there is to know about weddings: the traditional processional order, the best first dance songs, the latest trends in unity ceremonies and grand exits. And while that information is important to know, it does not tell you how to do the actual job! What you'll find in this book is practical, useful, applicable information on wedding coordination that was gained from real-life experience!

When I began, I had so many questions. Many of which I didn't even consider until a specific situation arose. Questions like "Is a wedding coordinator supposed to cut the cake if there's no one else to do it?" "What happens if the venue doesn't set up the tables and chairs? Does that become my responsibility?" "Is a wedding coordinator supposed to transport items?" "How many hours should I work on the actual wedding day?" "How many meetings should I have with my clients?" For my first few years as a wedding coordinator I was updating my contract after nearly every wedding I worked, strengthening my boundaries and redefining my role. All of these things that I learned, one wedding at a time, are now at your disposal! There are countless scenarios when it comes to weddings, and while it would be impossible to predict every scenario you might encounter, this book will provide you with an abundance of useful information that will not only help to solidify your understanding of the job, but will also set you up for success by putting you years ahead of the game!

In this book you will learn the ins and outs of wedding coordination. You will learn how a wedding coordinator differs from a wedding planner and why that distinction is important when defining your services. I will take you through the entire process of working with a client, beginning from the initial inquiry to that last hug at the end of a very successful wedding day! You will learn all about communicating with vendors and how best to handle those pesky wedding day mishaps! You will learn how to put together a foolproof wedding day timeline along with some solid time-saving setup tips! If you're anything like me (and you want to be a wedding coordinator so I'm sure you are), you want to know it all! Well let me assure you, as someone who is more than slightly detail-obsessed, I have included it *all* in this book! So, hunker down my friend and let's get started! Read on to learn everything you wanted to know (and a whole lot you didn't know you needed to know) about wedding coordination!

ONE

What is a Wedding Coordinator?

BEFORE WE DELVE INTO HOW THE JOB IS DONE, let's first focus on what, exactly, a wedding coordinator is! In short, a wedding coordinator is a professional who is hired by a couple to oversee their wedding day events, manage their team of vendors, and help to ensure the entire day runs smoothly and according to plan. Think wedding day fairy godmother! However, instead of a wand we have a clipboard, and instead of magical powers we have superhuman logistical awareness!

A WEDDING COORDINATOR'S RESPONSIBILITIES

A wedding coordinator has a long list of responsibilities, all of which are aimed at facilitating a seamless wedding day. While many of the responsibilities are dependent upon the details of each individual wedding, here are a few examples of a wedding coordinator's basic tasks:

- REVIEW THE CLIENT'S WEDDING PLANS AND ADDRESS ANY PROBLEMS
  - o If the client tells you that their flowers are being delivered, but the fine print on the contract is telling you otherwise, that's something you'll want to get worked out!

- PUT TOGETHER THE CLIENT'S WEDDING DAY TIMELINE
  - o Using various sources of information, you'll be able to expertly craft a fail-safe timeline for your clients so they don't end up with a three-hour long cocktail hour and a one-hour reception!

- ENSURE SETUP GOES AS PLANNED
  - o When a ceiling fan unexpectedly breaks at the venue, and instead of placing the table numbers you are now pushing tables aside to make room for the thirty-foot boom lift that is required to fix it, you'll need to be able to make some quick adjustments to your plan to ensure the venue is ready in time for the day's events!

- HANDLE VENDOR QUESTIONS AND CONCERNS
  - o The last thing you want is for the vendors to be hounding the bride with questions on her big day, so checking in with them frequently is imperative!

- MAKE SURE ALL NECESSARY ITEMS ARE IN PLACE
  - o Imagine in the middle of the ceremony it's time to light the unity candles and there is no lighter! Taking the

proper steps to ensure setup is complete will help to avoid oversights like this!

- MAKE SURE ANYONE WITH A SPECIAL ROLE IS PREPARED AND READY
  - When the MC introduces Uncle Bob for the dinner blessing, you want to be certain Uncle Bob is where he is supposed to be and not in line at the bar or off on a cigar break!

- KEEP THE RECEPTION EVENTS ON TRACK
  - If the events start falling behind, you could have a vendor run out of time, potentially causing your clients to miss out on some of the special moments they had planned for their wedding day!

WHAT WEDDING COORDINATORS ARE NOT

Wedding coordinators are many things: advisers, coaches, counselors, crisis managers, drill instructors (only when we have to be), and of course, organizational prodigies (obviously)! But here are a few things that wedding coordinators are not:

- WEDDING COORDINATORS ARE NOT WEDDING PLANNERS. While many wedding planners do offer wedding coordination services, the two roles have some notable differences. A wedding planner is, unsurprisingly, heavily involved in the *planning* of the wedding from beginning to end. A wedding planner often attends vendor meetings, tastings, dress fittings, etc. A wedding planner will have a large role in helping with the design, décor, layout, and overall look of the wedding spaces. Additionally, a wedding planner will likely be in charge of managing the wedding budget as well as the client's guest list. These are not typically tasks that a wedding coordinator gets involved with. Couples who hire a wedding coordinator do most of their own planning. They pick out and hire the vendors on their own, manage their own budget and guest list, handle food selections on their own, and take charge of their décor plans (for the most part). As a wedding coordinator, your job is to take those plans, fine-tune them, ensure the plans are unanimously understood by all parties, and make certain they happen!

- WEDDING COORDINATORS ARE NOT "ALL-IN-ONE" VENDORS. Don't get me wrong, a wedding coordinator will bend over backwards to ensure their client's wedding day is nothing less than perfect, and, in a predicament, may decide to jump outside their role and do the job of another vendor. However, as a general rule, it is not a wedding coordinator's job to take on the role of another vendor. For example, a wedding coordinator is not a DJ and should not be expected to emcee the wedding day. A wedding coordinator is not a caterer and should not be expected to slice the cake or clear the tables. A wedding coordinator is not a bartender and should never be asked to pour drinks. Be aware that some of these tasks carry bigtime liability issues! Now, in the spirit of full disclosure, I have to admit that I have been guilty of doing at least one (or maybe two) of these things. But that is why I have chosen to write this book, so you don't have to make the same mistakes I did! A wedding coordinator has a very demanding and important job to do, and spending time on these additional tasks can take away from their ability to effectively do their own job!

- WEDDING COORDINATORS ARE NOT VENUE COORDINATORS. Some venues come equipped with a venue coordinator. Venue coordinators are wonderful and can make your life a lot easier. They typically handle all venue-specific tasks, such as ensuring tables and chairs are properly set, managing in-house caterers or bartenders, and coordinating cleanup services. While venue coordinators can be incredibly helpful, they are not a replacement for a wedding coordinator. Keep in mind, venue coordinators work for the venue; wedding coordinators work for their clients! Venue coordinators, in general, do not contact the client's vendors or review contracts. They do not put together the timeline or offer setup assistance. They do not do all of the checks and preparations that wedding coordinators do all day long; it's just not their job. However, having a venue coordinator to work alongside you is a blessing! The more professionals you have working their magic behind the scenes, the better!

WHO HIRES A WEDDING COORDINATOR AND WHY?

Let's talk for a second about your potential clients. What types of couples hire wedding coordinators and why? There are two main reasons why this information is important to consider. One, knowing your target audience is a useful tool when it comes to marketing your business. Two, the answer to this question sets the framework for this entire book! Will all of your couples fall into one neat little category? No, absolutely not! Who would want that anyway? But there will be, in most cases, some commonalities among your clients. In general, your clients will be do-it-yourselfers and they will be budget conscious. You won't typically find yourself getting calls to coordinate weddings with a 500+ guest count, horse-drawn carriage processionals, pyrotechnics, and a helicopter grand entrance. That is more a job for a full-service wedding planner. You are likely to see more modest wedding plans from the couples who are seeking your services. With that being said, you will see some of the most inspiring creativity and heartwarming personal touches from your clients, and it will be truly rewarding to bring their plans to fruition.

Why do couples hire wedding coordinators? It's simple. They just want to enjoy their day! They want all of that stress, worry, and responsibility off of their shoulders so they are free to relax and focus on what the day is really about! That's where you come in!

CHALLENGES OF WEDDING COORDINATION

Wedding coordination is an amazing career! You get to meet so many great people and be a part of countless couples' best day ever. And you get the satisfaction of knowing that you had a huge role in making it all happen! However, there are also some challenging aspects of this job you should be aware of so you can be prepared to handle them when they arise.

- NOT ALL VENDORS WILL BE THRILLED TO WORK WITH YOU. Sometimes vendors get a little territorial. Sometimes they just don't like the idea of having someone tell them what to do (which isn't necessarily what you're there for, but how you may be viewed nonetheless). Whatever the reason may be, every now and then you'll run into a vendor who just doesn't like or respect your role, and may not respond to you in the most positive way (or even at all). Being acutely aware of this possibility, I always frame my communications with vendors using a "teamwork" approach. The goal is to convey that I'm not there to "take over" or micromanage them, but that I'm there to bring all of the different roles together into one cohesive and coordinated team effort. This approach definitely helps, but just know, you won't win everyone over every time and you'll just have to be OK with that. Be polite and respectful (read: professional) when handling any differences with vendors, but don't be afraid to inform them that you were hired by the couple to ensure things go according to plan, and that is all you are trying to do.

- YOU WILL OFTEN TAKE THE HEAT FOR OTHER PEOPLE'S DECISIONS. From the guests' perspective, you are oftentimes the one to be blamed for anything that displeases them! The guests don't like the seating assignment? Your fault. The caterer is running behind on refilling waters? Your fault. There is a terrible smell coming from the farm across the street? Yup, your fault! More often than not, guests will assume you are the wedding *planner* and will view you as the one who made all of the planning decisions. And while it may be hard at times, it's always best to handle these situations diplomatically. Simply say "I understand, I'll see what I can do," and go see what you can do. You can't fix every situation or make everyone happy, but when you can, you should! The couple has hired you to make their day as enjoyable as possible, and part of that means making sure the guests are happy too! Believe me, it's not always easy, but at the end of the day you can walk away knowing you did your best!

- SOMETIMES YOU WILL BE EXPECTED TO DO THINGS THAT ARE NOT YOUR JOB. I cannot stress enough how important it is to clearly define your boundaries and lay them all out right from the beginning. This will save you from having to deal with some misguided expectations and a whole lot of extra work! I once had a bride ask me, an hour before her ceremony, to paint a welcome sign (from scratch) and "figure out a way to hang it." Believe me, I have a hard time saying no to a bride on her wedding day, but on that day, in that situation, and with the mile-long list of things I was already dealing with, that was a hard no! It was an outrageous request and I simply just didn't have the time. The more straightforward you are about your services in the beginning, the fewer surprises and curveballs you will run into later on!

SKILLS OF A WEDDING COORDINATOR

It takes many different skills to be a great wedding coordinator. Many of them can be acquired with experience, but there are some important skills you should naturally possess when considering a career as a wedding coordinator.

- HIGHLY DETAIL-ORIENTED. Do you notice when a picture on the wall is just a hair off? Have you moved a decoration in your home a half an inch to the left, then a quarter inch to the right, and then just a millimeter back to the left? Do you space things out in perfect increments? Do you measure those spaces?? If you answered yes to any of these questions, then you are probably a detail-oriented person! Because a knife at a place setting on Table

20 that is pointed outward should stick out to you like a sore thumb!

- DIPLOMATIC. Should a conflict arise, you need to be able to effectively diffuse the tension and quickly come up with a solution that (hopefully) leaves all parties satisfied. Many conflicts arise from misunderstandings and poor communication. You'll often find that by simply explaining the situation from both perspectives, you'll be able to create a mutual understanding and (again, *hopefully*) an agreeable outcome. For example, during a wedding at a private residence, I once had an angry neighbor aggressively confront the mother of the bride because somebody had unintentionally parked in her driveway. After listening to the neighbor's frustrations, I learned that this happens to her almost every weekend and this time just happened to be the straw that broke the camel's back. I explained her position to the mother of the bride, who was initially upset at being unjustly yelled at. She was then a little more understanding of why the neighbor was so upset at this seemingly minor incident. We came up with a plan to prevent this from happening for the remainder of the event, both parties offered apologies and the day moved on seamlessly. Had I just dismissed the angry neighbor, things might have gone a little less desirably!

- DECISIVE. You'll need to make many on-the-spot decisions and oftentimes a lot will be riding on those decisions. One of the most difficult decisions you'll be called on to make is whether or not to utilize the rain plan for an outdoor ceremony (side note: you must insist on your couples having a rain plan)! You usually need to make this decision early on in the day (if not the day before) in order to ensure the site is set up on time, so the pressure is on to make the right call! You just have to use your best judgement, and every resource you can access, to make the most logical and educated decision that you can. If your decision, for whatever reason, doesn't go over well with your clients, simply explain why you felt that decision was best and that you truly had their best interests in mind. More often than not, they will understand.

- HARD WORKING. Let me introduce you to the term "wedding hangover." The first time I heard this term in the industry I was shocked! I thought, "You guys are drinking on the job!? So much so that you are regularly getting a hangover!??" I quickly learned that a "wedding hangover" has nothing to do with alcohol. It is a term used to describe how wedding professionals feel in the days following a wedding, much like an actual hangover! Twelve hours straight of nonstop hustling, plus too few bathroom breaks, plus insufficient intake of food and water, plus the general stress of managing a wedding equals... a wedding hangover! Working a wedding is both physically and mentally demanding, and you need to have the drive and work ethic to stick with it from beginning to end!

- RESOURCEFUL. Any good wedding coordinator wouldn't leave home without their fully stocked emergency wedding kit, but sometimes even we are presented with a technical challenge that can't be solved by opening up our majestic supply case. In these situations, you must channel your inner MacGyver! In other words, find a creative and clever way to fix the problem. For example, I was once attaching seating assignment cards to a door using clothespins and twine. This free-standing, decorative door was placed on the venue's back deck. While attempting to clip one of the cards, the clothespin broke and the card slipped right between two deck boards! There was no way to get under the deck to recover the card, so I had to get creative! I ended up cutting a long strip of cardboard from a box and attached a thin piece of rolled-up duct tape to the end of it. I was able to bring the card close enough to the surface to reach in with my needle-nose plyers and grab it! Had I not been so resourceful, the beautifully calligraphed escort card would have been gone forever and replaced with a napkin and a sharpie!

- CONFIDENT. This is a big one! Self-doubt will not serve you well in this business. You don't have to possess *all* of the confidence in the world, your self-assurance will increase with experience, but you should be able to portray confidence in a way that fosters trust from your clients. You want them to view you as someone who will knock their wedding out of the park (or barn, or greenhouse... or airport hangar)! If you doubt yourself, others will doubt you as well. The best way to build confidence is to know your job inside and out. And guess what! You're on the right track! Hopefully by the end of this book you'll be brimming with confidence and knowledge, ready to take on that first job and totally nail it!

WEDDING COORDINATION OR WEDDING MANAGEMENT?

If you're familiar with the term "day-of coordination," which I'm guessing you probably are, you might be wondering why I haven't been using it. There's a reason! Although the term is still commonly used, it is considered among many in the industry to be, at best, misleading. It tends to give potential clients an oversimplified idea of what the service actually is, not only undermining its value to the client, but also grossly downplaying the amount of work that goes into this service. So, while many planners and coordinators are still using the term "day-of coordination," others have transitioned into calling it simply "wedding coordination." Some have abandoned the old term entirely and are instead labeling the service "wedding management." Whether you prefer "coordination" or "management," I highly recommend avoiding the "day-of" terminology. It's unnecessary, it's confusing, and it's inaccurate. Save yourself the hassle of having to repeatedly explain why "day-of coordination" is more than just a "one-day job," and do what the industry is currently doing: drop it like it's hot!

Understanding the role of a wedding coordinator is an important first step in learning the job. Knowing ahead of time which tasks you *should* be doing, and which tasks you should stay away from, saves you from having to learn the hard way! In addition, this information lays the groundwork for learning the process of working with clients. In the next chapter, you will learn everything about wedding coordination, from responding to client inquiries to successfully managing a client's wedding day!

TWO

Working With Clients

THERE ARE MANY POTENTIAL VARIATIONS to the process of working with clients, and not all wedding coordinators will go about their service in the exact same way. Some, for example, prefer to have one meeting with their clients, while others find it more beneficial to have two or more. Some wedding coordinators will include twelve hours of wedding day service, while others might only include eight. It will be up to you to determine your own unique process, but to get you started, I have laid out the basic steps for working with clients.

- THE INQUIRY
  - A couple reaches out to you to express interest in your services and requests more information.

- THE CONSULTATION
  - The consultation is your opportunity to learn more about the couple's needs, plans, personalities, and expectations, as well as your opportunity to share with the couple how you can make their wedding day the best that it can be!

- THE CONTRACT AND DEPOSIT
  - Once a couple decides they would like to hire you, you will need to seal the deal with a signed contract to ensure that all arrangements and expectations are mutually agreed upon by both parties.

- CLIENT ONBOARDING
  - Client onboarding involves familiarizing new clients with your business policies and practices, and providing useful information and tools to help facilitate your working relationship.

- COMMUNICATION AND GATHERING INFORMATION
  - During this time, you will gather and collect all wedding related information from your clients in order to fully understand their wedding day plans and goals.

- THE QUESTIONNAIRE
  - The questionnaire is your tool for gathering the most pertinent information on your client's wedding day expectations. It will help to ensure that your clients have thought through every detail of their day.

- THE MEETING
    - During your meeting (or meetings if you choose to offer more than one) you will review everything you've learned so far about your client's wedding plans and follow up on any areas that were previously unclear or undecided.

- COMMUNICATING WITH VENDORS AND BUILDING THE TIMELINE
    - With the information you have gathered thus far, you can begin piecing together your client's timeline and reaching out to vendors to confirm all of the plans and arrangements, as well as answer any lingering questions the wedding vendors may have.

- THE REHEARSAL
    - Whether you're facilitating the rehearsal yourself, or in tandem with the officiant, your goal is to ensure all parties involved in the ceremony fully understand their role. This includes placement, cues, timing, and any assigned duties.

- THE WEDDING DAY
    - It's time to put all of the plans into action!

THE INQUIRY

Whether it's through your website, a wedding planning site, or by direct email, potential clients will express their interest in your services by reaching out to you to request more information. You may simply have nothing more than a name, email address, and a wedding date, but little is more exciting than having a brand-new potential client ringing your proverbial doorbell! The first thing to think about is whether you'll respond by phone or by email. My go-to method is always an email response. I find that by offering a thorough explanation of my services along with an upfront quote of my fee, I am essentially saving both myself and the potential client time and energy by laying it all out there right from the beginning. If they like it and want to move forward, great! If not, then it's not what they are looking for and that's fine too! This approach works well for me, but you may find a different tactic that better fits your personality. See Appendix A for a sample response to an inquiry from a prospective new client.

PRO TIP: Do your best to respond to inquiries within one business day. A quick response sends the message that you are not only excited about the possibility of working with them, but that you also respect their time! This helps to make a great first impression!

THE CONSULTATION

A potential client has reached out to you and you've responded with a description of your services and your fee. They like what they've learned so far and want to move forward. What happens next? In order to exchange more in-depth information with this potential client, you'll need to set up a consultation. This is a very critical step in the process. This is where you get clients! Without clients, there is no business, and nothing else in this book will matter! There is a lot that goes into a successful consultation, and a lot riding on it, so get comfortable because there is much to learn!

Let's start by talking about the goals of the consultation. Ultimately, your goal is to get the couple to hire you, but it goes a little deeper than that. Your first goal is to ensure that the couple fully understands your services and has no misconceptions about what wedding coordination is, and what it is not! Your second goal is to ensure that you have a basic understanding of the couple's general plans and wishes, to be certain their needs align with your services. The goal of the consultation, therefore, is to ensure that you are not only a good fit for them, but that they are also a good fit for you!

Every now and then you may have a potential client so eager to book you that they want to skip the consultation entirely! While it may be tempting to accept the job, I would advise against it. Imagine blindly accepting a job only to find out that the couple wants to include all twenty-seven of their cats in the wedding processional, each dressed in little cat suspenders and cat bowties! I'd take an invitation to this wedding any day of the week, but to coordinate this logistical nightmare... no thanks! I realize that's a dramatic example, but my point is that you need to ensure that it's a good fit all around. I'm not here to tell you to turn down jobs, but if something doesn't feel right, trust your instincts! It's OK to tell a client that you don't feel that you are the best fit for that job. In the beginning, I completely ignored that instinct and ended up regretting it! I've had some very challenging jobs that I could sense from the beginning were going to be so, but I moved forward anyway and got put through the wringer! If you're getting a bad vibe, trust yourself. Maybe it's just a style you're not gelling with; maybe it sounds too challenging for your experience level; maybe you're getting a bridezilla vibe, I don't know! Whatever the case may be, don't be afraid to turn it down and offer some referrals.

How will your consultation take place? Will it be over the phone? Will it be in person? Will you offer video calling? Will you have a set policy on this or will you let the potential client decide? More often than not, my consultations occur over the phone as a good majority of my clients are from out of state. However, if a couple requests that the consultation be in person, I do my best to accommodate. I actually much prefer the in-person consultations because it is so nice to begin to build that connection right from the beginning. However, I have absolutely no problems with the over-the-phone consultations. It just comes down to personal preference and logistics.

What do you talk about in a consultation? A good place to start is to have the couple give you a brief rundown of where they are in the planning process. Which vendors have they hired and which vendors do they still need to hire? What do they envision for their day? What kind of atmosphere, or feel, are they going for (formal, casual, backyard cookout, festival, etc.)? What are the general event time frames (ceremony, cocktail hour, reception, etc.)? Some important questions you want to be sure to ask during your consultation are:

- What is the estimated guest count?
- What time is the ceremony and where?
- What time will the reception start and where?
- What time do you have access to the venue? By what time must everyone be out?
- What is the general plan for décor?

Some important information you want to share (or reiterate) with the couple is:

- What's included and what's not included in your services
- Your general process for working with clients
- Your wedding day hours of service
- Payment schedule and accepted forms of payment

I suggest limiting your consultation to no more than an hour, and be sure to set this expectation early on when the consultation is scheduled. Your time is valuable and so is your knowledge, be mindful of how and where you spend it! While it is beneficial to share a few snippets of your knowledge, be careful not to get caught up in giving away too much free advice! Occasionally, a couple will ask you for a vendor referral. There are some varying opinions out there among wedding planners and coordinators on whether or not to offer up vendor referrals *before* being hired. Personally, I don't find it to be a big issue to offer a vendor referral or two in the consultation. However, if I'm starting to get the feel that the couple is just after some free wedding planning, then I'll quickly steer the conversation back to discussing the services I offer "once hired."

At the end of the consultation, you'll want to discuss the next steps in the process if they decide they would like to move forward in hiring you as their wedding coordinator. Sometimes you'll get hired on the spot, other times they'll let you know the next day, or even sometimes the next week. Or sometimes you just never hear from them again, and that's OK! Regardless of the outcome, you should always try to reflect on your performance, identify areas where you could use a little fine-tuning, and come up with a plan to help yourself improve!

PRO TIP: Create an outline or mini-questionnaire to use during your consultations to help keep you on track! With as much information as there is to share during the consultation, the conversation can easily take its own path. Having a questionnaire to follow will help to ensure that you walk away with all of the information you need! See Appendix B for a sample consultation questionnaire.

I know from experience that the consultation can be a little nerve-wrecking. Self-promoting, much like you would in a job interview, is not the easiest thing to do! It can feel a little uncomfortable to talk yourself up and try to convince someone that they need to hire you! This is where the ability to portray confidence really becomes vital. Another important determinant of your success will be your ability to connect with the potential client. Finding commonalities between you and the potential client is a great way to build a connection, especially if it's something non-wedding related! Are you both dog people? Nature lovers? Foodies? Netflix bingers? The more common ground you can bring to light, the more likely they are to entrust you with their wedding vision. In other words, the more they view your personality as like their own, the more comfortable they will feel having *you* as their wedding day representative!

THE CONTRACT AND DEPOSIT

Congratulations! You've nailed the consultation and the couple wants to hire you! Now you must solidify the arrangement with a contract. Creating your contract can seem like an arduous and overwhelming task, but with all of the resources available out there, you will have your contract whipped together in no time! Both www.rocketlawyer.com and www.legalzoom.com have some great resources for creating a small business contract. You can also find contract templates specific to wedding planners on www.plannerslounge.com. Once you have drafted your contract, you'll want to have a business lawyer review it to ensure you are not missing any crucial elements. Here are some basic items you'll want to be sure to include in your contract:

- Your name, business name, and your job title
- Your clients' full names
- Your clients' contact information (phone, email, and/or home address)
- Date services will begin and end
- Dates and locations of specific events you agree to attend (i.e. rehearsal, ceremony, and reception)
- Events, actions, or conditions that would terminate the agreement
- Description of the services you will provide
- Your duties and responsibilities
- The clients' duties and responsibilities
- The fee and payment schedule
- A list of conditions that would alter the fee, if any
- Accepted forms of payment
- Late payment/nonpayment policy
- Cancellation policy
- Stipulations for making any changes to the contract

When it comes to delivering the contract to your clients, you have a few options. You can send a hard copy in the mail, email a copy, or use a program that allows your clients to view and sign the contract electronically. Using the e-sign option is the fastest and simplest method, particularly for the client, but often involves a fee. If you're looking to avoid additional fees as you begin building your business, emailing the contract is a good second option. Whatever format you have your contract in, just be sure that it is unmodifiable. Using a PDF or read-only file will help safeguard against any unauthorized contract adjustments.

Along with the signed contract, you should also be collecting a deposit (or retainer) to be able to secure your client's wedding date. Anywhere up to half of your total fee is an acceptable requirement for the deposit. The deposit not only serves as proof that your client is truly serious about hiring you, but also protects you from losing out on income should your client decide to terminate the contract. Let's say you accept the job with only a signed contract and no upfront payment, then a month before the wedding, your client decides to elope in Italy! All of the work you've put in up to that point could potentially go uncompensated! Your deposit is your safeguard from nonpayment.

Once you have the signed contract, and the deposit has been received, you'll want to put together a folder, or binder, to keep yourself organized! A simple two-pocket folder works great for me; I find it to be more travel-friendly than a binder. However, a binder can be a bit tidier and better organized. In addition, you'll also want to create a file folder on your computer as a backup. Be sure to keep your folder and file labels consistent. Create a client folder for each year ("2019 Clients" or "2020 Clients") and within each year, create a folder for each client. You can choose to label each client folder using first names ("Lynette & Becca") or last names ("Winters & Perez"). Within each client's file folder, you'll want to keep your document titles as simple as possible (e.g. "Photographer Contract" or "DJ Questionnaire"). Keeping things simple and consistent will help to ensure you are well organized and always on top of your game!

CLIENT ONBOARDING

You officially have a new client! Time for a happy dance! A short happy dance, of course, because you've got work to do! The next step in the process is known as client onboarding. Onboarding is essentially the process of welcoming a new client into the business, informing them of your basic policies, and sharing useful tools that will help them get the most out of their time with you. You'll want to create an onboarding kit (or welcome packet) to share with each new client you acquire. You can purchase premade templates online or choose to create your own! Whichever option you choose, be sure to put some thought into the look of the packaging and material in order to stay consistent with your brand (you'll learn more about building your brand in Chapter 3). Most welcome packets are housed in a fancy folder, but feel free to get creative with your packaging! If you choose to use a business management site for your business, such as HoneyBook or Aisle Planner, you can opt to create a completely digital welcome packet that can be delivered automatically to your client's inbox upon signing the contract. Whichever option you prefer, aim for the "wow factor" when putting together your welcome packet material. Not only will your clients be impressed, but they will feel even more confident in their decision to work with you! Here are some basic items to include in your welcome packet:

- Office policies
  - o Business hours
  - o Contact info
    - Phone number
    - Email address
    - Mailing address
  - o Payment information
    - Accepted forms of payment
    - What name to put on a check
  - o Meeting policies
    - When to schedule meetings
    - Where meetings can take place
    - Cancellation policy
  - o Communication guidelines
    - Ways to communicate with you
    - When to expect a response from you
- Copy of the contract
- Social media card
- Hand-written thank you card

In addition to the basic information listed above, you can go a step further for your clients and include some helpful documents, such as:

- A checklist of items to bring on the wedding day
- A list of songs commonly used for specialty dances
- Décor prepping tips or requirements (see Appendix C)
- A list of traditional and nontraditional unity ceremony ideas
- Tips on writing your own vows
- A list of things to do after getting married

PRO TIP: Add a little flair to your welcome packets by packing some confetti inside or tying ribbon around the outside that matches your clients' wedding colors!

COMMUNICATION AND GATHERING INFORMATION

The next step in the process is opening up communication between you and your client and gathering information. This includes collecting vendor contracts, basic event timeframes, and general décor plans. At this point, you could be anywhere from two months to one year out from the wedding, so you will have some decisions to make on your policy regarding your clients' access to you. Will you offer unlimited communication to your clients right from the beginning or hold off on the communication until a set date (typically something along the lines of eight to twelve weeks from the wedding date)? Some coordinators like to be available to their clients right from the beginning and offer unlimited communication (calls, emails, maybe even text messaging) from the point the contract is signed. This really goes over well with potential clients as it provides them with some comfort knowing they can ask questions and get advice throughout the remainder of their planning process. It's a great selling point for your business. However, it does mean that you will be putting more hours (potentially *significantly* more hours) into some jobs versus others, with no difference in compensation. There is also a very fine line between offering guidance as a coordinator and inadvertently turning into a virtual planner, and it can be difficult for the client to understand the distinction. On the other hand, it can be advantageous to be involved in earlier communication with your client, as this often leads to a more in-depth understanding of their wedding plans and vendor arrangements, giving you a greater chance at identifying any and all areas of weakness.

Another option to consider is to stipulate that while you can be booked at any time, your service does not begin until a set date. This helps to ensure that all of your clients are getting the same level of service from you, and that you are being fairly compensated for the work you are putting in. This also helps to keep your workload more balanced and predictable. Additionally, gathering information much closer to the wedding date (as opposed to ten, eleven, or even twelve months out) means that the information you receive from your clients will be more reliable and less likely to change. It also helps to ensure that the majority of the planning is done by the client and that you are not getting pulled into that role.

A third option is to offer limited communication (e.g. a set number of emails, or a specific number of questions) up until a set date, and then provide unlimited communication from that point on. With this option, you are still offering support to your clients during their planning stage, but you are forcing them to be selective with their requests. This allows you to have more control over the number of hours you will spend on each job. Some jobs will naturally require a little more work than others, but putting a cap on your communication will prevent this from getting out of hand. Whichever policy you decide on, keep it consistent among all of your clients. If, after some time and experience, you decide that a particular policy is not working out well, don't be afraid to make a change. Just be sure you are sticking to the original policy with any current clients who have signed their contract under those conditions, and implementing the change with new clients who hire you from that point forward. Be aware that any new potential clients could be referrals from past clients, and they may expect to get the same policy and services that your previous client did. Should this come up, simply offer a brief explanation of the new policy, and the reason behind it, and stand your ground. You cannot make exceptions to your policy for some clients and not others. Being inconsistent is not good business practice. The same goes for any changes in your pricing. The couple can decide, based on your *current* service terms, whether or not they feel your services are the best fit for their needs. In addition to providing fair and consistent service to all of your clients, you need to ensure you are being fair to yourself as well! It may take a little experience, and a little trial and error, but in time you will find what works best for you and for your business.

Now the time has come to get your feet wet! Where do you start? The first thing you'll want to do is to collect copies of every single contract your client has signed with their vendors. I know this seems obvious, but make sure the copy you receive is actually filled out with your client's information and signed. I have, indeed, had clients send me blank contracts before! Additionally, you should be requesting copies of any forms or questionnaires the client has filled out for other vendors. Your goal here is to ensure that your clients are providing consistent information all around. Wedding planning is an enormous undertaking that most clients have zero experience with, and they often don't realize how important the tiny details are. Occasionally, a client might inadvertently give you information that is different from the information they gave to another vendor. Keep in mind, sometimes couples are filling out these various forms for their vendors months before you arrive in the picture, so they often forget some of the specific details they previously provided, or maybe have adjusted their plans at some point and forgot to share the updates. For example, let's say the couple specifies to you the order in which they want the wedding party introduced for the grand entrance, but unknowingly gave the DJ a slightly different order. It's time to do the introductions and you're sending couples through the doors while the DJ is announcing the wrong names! Embarrassing, right? We want to avoid that! By crosschecking all of the information you are given, you are able to catch these inconsistencies early on, limiting (or preventing entirely) those wedding day blunders!

As the contracts begin to roll in, you'll want to keep track of the information you have received using a "Vendor Contact Sheet" (see Appendix D). This document will not only serve as a quick reference for each vendor's contact information, but will also help you to easily identify any missing information so you can be sure to request it from your client! Your template should include a list of all of the most commonly used vendor categories (venue, photographer, florist, bakery, etc.) plus a few extra spaces, labeled "other," for some of the less common vendor categories that you'll come across every once in a while (magician, harpist, ice-cream truck, etc.). Include space for each hired vendor's business name and contact information (main contact name, number, email, and/or website), and a box to check once you have received a copy of the contract. When the client asks you, "Am I forgetting anything?", you'll be able to look right at this sheet to easily answer that question!

Next, you will learn about reviewing vendor contracts. First, you'll need a few items. In addition to the contract itself, you'll need a pen, a highlighter, and some sticky notes. What are you looking for? Cold, hard facts!

- Vendor contact info (name, phone number, email address, website)

- Locations, dates, and times of service
- Exact service provided and vendor's responsibilities
- Start times, end times, and hours of service
- Any responsibilities required of the couple
- List of items the vendor is providing, if any (should include total numbers, colors, or other descriptive terms)
- Special requirements, such as:
  - Meal specifications
  - Break times
  - Items needed for service (tables, chairs, extension cords, etc.)
  - Space requirements
  - Technical requirements (lighting, internet access, outlets, etc.)

As you read through each contract, you'll want to highlight all relevant details. At this point, you will want to focus mostly on information that is specific to the wedding day. For example, you won't need to worry about upcoming payments, meetings, or due dates, as those are the responsibility of the client. In addition, keep an eye out for any missing information. If there are any details you need, or questions that arise, you'll want to write them down on the sticky notes and attach them to the contract. When it's time to begin communicating with the vendors, you will be well prepared!

PRO TIP: Although you are not responsible for handling your clients' vendor payments or scheduling their meetings, you *may* wish to include reminders for upcoming tasks as part of your

> service. Remember, the more you do to keep your
> clients on track, the smoother everything will go for
> you!

You will come across contracts of all kinds, from fully-detailed ten-page documents to a mere two-sentence agreement with a signature. Sometimes you'll need a little information; sometimes you'll need a lot! Whatever the case, you need to be certain that you are filling in *all* of the missing pieces. No matter how obvious something may seem, you simply can never assume anything! Making an assumption, and being wrong, can be a very costly mistake. If it's not spelled out in fully-indisputable detail, you'll need to get clarification from the vendor. The following are examples of assumptions gone wrong:

- I once assumed that since the caterer was providing the dinnerware, that they would also be the ones in charge of setting it all out. They were not.
- I assumed that the florist, who was driving across state lines for the event, would take into account the time change when planning her arrival time. She did not.
- I assumed that the linens provided by the venue would not look like they just came out of a college kid's hamper! They did.
- And lastly, I assumed that the bartenders, who provided the drinks, would be responsible for clearing the hundreds of glasses that were left on the tables. Oh, they most certainly were not!

You have to ask *all* of the questions. And yes, vendors will get annoyed with you, and yes, it can feel a little embarrassing to ask a caterer, "You are providing plates, right?" But believe me, it is so much better than discovering on the wedding day that the caterer does not provide the plates!

In addition to the items previously mentioned, here are some vendor-specific details you'll want to look for on the contract:

- PHOTOGRAPHER/VIDEOGRAPHER
  - How many photographers/videographers will be shooting the wedding?
  - Is there an additional fee for shooting multiple locations?

- DJ/BAND
  - Which events are they booked for (just ceremony, just reception, or all events)?
  - How many DJ's or band members will there be?

- HAIR/MAKEUP
  - How many stylists/artists will be providing services?
  - By what time are the services expected to be finished?
  - What is the estimated time needed per person?
  - Will they be creating a specific schedule for the group or will it be determined on the wedding day?
  - What forms of payment will be accepted on the wedding day?

- CATERERS
  - How many staff members will be working?
  - Which items will they be responsible for setting up and when will that begin?
  - What are their end-of-night responsibilities? Which items are they responsible for clearing/cleaning at the end of the night?

- o   What is their policy for leftover food? Do they discard it, offer to donate it, or package it up for the clients to take home?

- BARTENDERS
  - o   How many staff members will be working?
  - o   Are they responsible for clearing cups/glasses?
  - o   What is the policy for when something runs out? Is there a fee associated with this?
  - o   What happens with leftover alcohol? Do the clients get to keep any opened bottles?

- VENUE
  - o   By what time does the music need to end?
  - o   Are there any décor restrictions (no candles, no affixing to walls/ceiling, no outside plants, no confetti/bubbles/ flower petals, etc.)?
  - o   Do they require event insurance?
  - o   Are there any non-standard policies you need to be aware of (no moving tables, no garbage left in garbage bins, no "shots" of alcohol allowed, etc.)?
  - o   Are there any venue restrictions you should be aware of (no heating or air conditioning, limited parking available, no running water or drinking water, etc.)?
  - o   What is the building maximum capacity?
  - o   Does the venue take care of setting up and taking down tables and chairs?
  - o   Will a venue staff member be on-site during the event?

- o What would cause the clients to lose their security deposit, if a deposit was required?
- o Are vehicles allowed to remain on the property overnight? If so, by what date/time are they required to be removed?

- FLORIST
  - o Are they providing delivery and setup services? If so, what time?
  - o What needs to be set up before their arrival (tables, linens, arch, etc.)?
  - o Will they be returning at the end of the night to tear down?
  - o What is the return policy for any rented items?

- OFFICIANT
  - o Will they attend the rehearsal?
  - o When do they prefer to be given the marriage license (at the rehearsal or on the wedding day)?
  - o Will the officiant be responsible for getting the marriage license to the county or governing entity?

- BAKERY
  - o Are they delivering the cake or other desserts? If so, are they also setting up?
  - o Are they providing a cake stand or dessert trays? If so, what is the return policy?

- TRANSPORTATION
  - o What are the pickup times and locations?
  - o What are the drop-off times and locations?

o   Are there any planned stops?

o   Does the vehicle stay on-site in between trips?

o   Is there a policy in the case of a vehicle breakdown?

o   Is there a policy for bringing alcoholic beverages onto
    the vehicle?

In addition to the contracts, here are some other documents you can request from your clients (your clients may not yet have these items, but on the off chance they do, you'll want a copy):

- Venue floor plans (ceremony, cocktail hour, and reception)
- Seating assignments
- Ceremony outline

THE QUESTIONNAIRE

In order to successfully manage your client's wedding day from beginning to end, you'll need much more information than what you'll find on the contracts. This is where your questionnaire comes in! Your questionnaire is the tool you will use to ensure every aspect of your client's wedding day is well thought out and thoroughly planned. It should cover everything from your client's morning plans to how they are leaving the venue at the end of the night! It should be designed to focus on all of the nitty-gritty details. Does the couple want their wedding party introduced by full names, first names only, or nicknames? Would they prefer to cut the cake before the first dance or after? Will their wedding party walk down the aisle in pairs or individually? The sample questionnaire provided in this book illustrates just how in-depth and thorough your questionnaire should be (see Appendix E). Remember, your goal is to know as much as you possibly can about what your clients want for their day. In fact, as the wedding coordinator, it's your job to know! Because if a vendor, a guest, or even a member of the wedding party has a question, it's you they will be asking!

When is the best time to send the questionnaire to your clients? This is entirely up to you! You can send it right away once you've been hired, or wait until a set number of weeks from the wedding date. Sending the questionnaire out early on can be helpful to the client and provide some much-needed guidance. While this may be beneficial to some clients, it could actually be overwhelming to others who aren't quite ready to think about those intricate details just yet! It works well for me to send the questionnaire around eight weeks prior to the wedding date. Whether you decide to send the questionnaire earlier or later, the more important piece to consider is when you will want the questionnaire returned to you! I would suggest having your clients submit their questionnaire to you by no less than three business days prior to your meeting (perhaps even a full week before the meeting in the early stages of your business). This allows you adequate time to review their responses, formulate your follow-up questions, and get yourself fully prepared for the meeting.

There are a number of different ways in which you can create and share your questionnaire. You can simply create a document using a standard word processor, such as Microsoft Word or Apple Pages. If you're using this method, I would suggest converting the file to a PDF before sending it to your clients. They can then choose how they want to fill in their responses and return the form to you. Whether they type in their answers and email it back to you, or print it out, handwrite their responses and send it in the mail, your client can use whichever method best fits their technical savviness! Another option is to use an online program that provides various business management tools (e.g. contracts, questionnaires, checklists, etc.) all in a digital format. Websites such as www.17hats.com or www.aisleplanner.com (the latter being a platform specifically for wedding professionals) can be a one-stop shop for all of your business management needs! These conveniences, however, do not come without a cost, so you'll need to decide on whether or not they benefit your business enough to be worth the additional expense.

Once the client has submitted their completed questionnaire to you, you can begin reviewing it. Time to bring back the sticky notes! Much like reviewing contracts, you are looking for any missing pieces of information as well as areas where you may need a little clarification. Also, if there are any areas that you feel could use a little improving or reevaluating, you'll want to make note of those as well! For example, let's say the client indicates that their hair and makeup is set to be done by 2:00 p.m. and the ceremony is set to begin at 2:30 p.m. However, they've also indicated that they plan on doing a first look with their photographer before the ceremony. This would be an area you'd want to address. Thirty minutes is not enough time to get into a dress, coordinate the first look, get the photos, and then get everyone lined up and ready for the 2:30 p.m. ceremony. Sticky note that for sure!

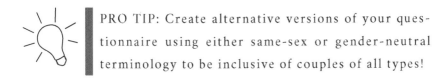

PRO TIP: Create alternative versions of your questionnaire using either same-sex or gender-neutral terminology to be inclusive of couples of all types!

THE MEETING

Some coordinators include one meeting in their package while others feel they benefit more from having two meetings. This will be something that you will have to come to a decision on based on experience. Use your best judgement to come up with a starting policy, taking into consideration all factors (time, travel, expenses, etc.), and give it a try! For me, I find it sufficient to conduct one longer meeting (up to three hours) three to five weeks prior to the wedding date. Any follow up I have afterwards is done via phone or email. You may find this works for you as well, or you may find that offering two shorter meetings, a month or so apart, works better for you and your clients.

It is always helpful to hold your meeting at the venue whenever possible. This way you can discuss the layout and optional floor plans as well as identify any space-related constraints. However, sometimes meeting at the venue is just not an option due to a venue-specific policy or simply a timing issue. If that's the case, you can meet at a nearby coffee shop, restaurant, or even a park (weather permitting). If the meeting cannot be held at the venue, you should make it a point to visit the venue at another time (preferably before the meeting).

In order to make the most of your face time with your clients, you need to spend some time preparing for your meeting! A day or two before your scheduled meeting, gather all of the information you have received from your clients thus far and review it all! Reread through all prior correspondence, all contracts, and the questionnaire. Make a list of any additional information or documents you still need. Using the information you have, begin piecing together a basic timeline for your client's wedding day. Include as many of the following components as possible:

- Venue access time
- Hair/makeup start and end times
- Vendor arrival times
- Transportation times

- First look time and location
- Ceremony attendants' line up time and order
- Ceremony start time
- Processional order and songs
- Ceremony order of events
- Ceremony end time
- Recessional order and song
- Cocktail hour start time
- Any specified photography times
- Grand entrance line up time
- Grand entrance order and songs
- Blessing and toast times
- Dinner start time
- First dance time
- Special dance times
- Open dancing start time
- Cake cutting time
- Bouquet/garter toss times
- Last call time
- DJ/Band end time
- Vendor end times
- Cleanup schedule
- Venue close time

Your goal here is to lay out the basic structure of their day. Not all of this information will be available to you at this point, but most of it should! Once you have the basic timeline down, review it! Look for any areas where there may not be enough time allotted, or perhaps too much time allotted, and write down some suggested adjustments. Also, your client won't likely have listed specific times for a majority of these events, but you'll be able to figure out an estimated time for most events based on the information you *do* have.

Once you have all of your items prepared, pack them up in the order in which you'll be reviewing them with your client. Not only will this help keep you on track during the meeting, but will also keep you from looking unorganized! You'll have exactly what you need, right when you need it!

Depending upon your process, the meeting could be the first time you actually get to see your clients in person! Keep in mind, it may not be *just* your clients! You might also be meeting with Mom, Sister, Maid of Honor, or anyone else they wanted to bring along for support. Think about whether or not you'll want to implement a policy here to limit the number of extra people at the meeting. The more people there are, the more debating there will be over decisions, and the longer the meeting will go! I would suggest allowing no more than two additional support people to attend the meeting along with your clients. Be sure your clients know ahead of time that the only decisions you will implement are the ones made by the clients themselves, and that their guests are there for support only. This can get a little tricky if someone other than your client is paying for your services. They may feel this gets them some leverage in making decisions. To help avoid this, I specify in my contract that regardless of who pays the fee, I take instruction from the couple only.

It's finally time for the meeting! If your meeting will take place at the venue, you'll want to start with a quick walk-through of the space. As you walk around, talk about where your client envisions the placement of various items (e.g. the dessert table, the band, the gift table, etc.). Some venues will have more options than others. If you were given a floor plan already, take notes on it! If you don't yet have one, make a quick sketch of the room on the back of a piece of paper. As much as you think you'll remember everything they tell you, chances are you won't! Do yourself a huge favor and write it down! Here are some things you'll want to discuss during your walk-through of the venue:

- Placement of all tables, including food tables (appetizer table, buffet tables, dessert table, etc.) and specialty tables (welcome table, gifts/cards table, wedding favors table, etc.)
- DJ and/or band placement (pay attention to any load-in requirements or challenges)
- Ceremony location, cocktail hour location, and reception location and layouts
- Ideas for where you could line up the wedding party and possibly where the bride could be hidden (if not doing a first look)
- Where boxes, bins, or tubs can be stored after setup

PRO TIP: If the venue is low on storage space, store empty decor bins and boxes under specialty tables (as long as the linens are floor length)! This way, you'll also have quick and easy access to them at the end of the night when it's time to pack up.

After you've had a little time to get familiar with the venue and the couple's design preferences, you'll then want to sit down with your clients and review the questionnaire. Start from the beginning and work your way through all of your questions. Get clarification where you need it and offer advice where your clients may need it. If your clients are struggling with a particular decision, help them work through it. Discuss the pros and cons of each option and maybe even suggest an alternative solution. Point out any foreseeable challenges and help them smooth those out. As you go through your meeting, keep a list of any tasks you give them. For example, if you've asked the couple to email you an updated floor plan or get you their song selections, you'll want to write that down. That way you can be certain that you did, in fact, request these items, and it will help you keep track of what information you still need!

After you've gone through the questionnaire, you should review all of the vendor contracts with your client. Have there been any changes or updates to the contracts since you received a copy? Is there any vendor contact information that is missing from the contract that your client can share with you (perhaps an email address or phone number)? When it comes to clarifying information pertaining to the vendors and their responsibilities, it is best to hear it from the client first! For example, if it's not clear on the contract what color the table runners should be, you'll want to ask the client first before reaching out to the vendor. This way, you will always know what the client wants and be able to confirm that information with the vendor.

Once you've reviewed the contracts, you will then want to go over the general timeline for the day. Your goal here is to make sure you fully understand your client's preferred order of events, as well as to ensure your clients have given adequate thought to their preferences! Sometimes, clients make decisions on their day based solely on the belief that there is no other way of doing things, so it's always a good idea to have a conversation about how they came to their decisions and perhaps offer some alternative ideas for them to think about! Maybe they've only ever been to one wedding, and at *that* wedding the couple had their first dance after their grand entrance. So, assuming that's just how it's done, your client has listed that as their preference. Maybe after discussing other options with you, they realize they would much prefer to do their first dance after dinner, or maybe they don't really want to do a first dance at all! I always encourage clients to do what they want for their wedding day, whether it's following tradition or throwing it out the window. It's their day; every second of it should represent who they are! However, if they *are* deviating from tradition, you'll want to be sure they *know* they are, and that it was their intent to do so. Let's say your client indicates on the questionnaire that they want to include the parents in the processional, but have listed the mother of the bride to walk first, and the parents of the groom to walk second. Traditionally, the mother of the bride would be the last non-wedding party member to walk down the aisle, indicating the official beginning of the ceremony. In this case, you'll want to be certain that the switch from tradition was intentional and not simply accidental. In some groups, this may not be much of an issue. In others, however, it could cause some significantly hurt feelings!

To wrap up your meeting, you'll want to talk about what happens next. Discuss with your client the plans for contacting the vendors. It's normal during the meeting to unearth a lot of questions that need to be worked out, leaving some clients eager to reach out to their vendors to get some answers! You'll want to avoid having both you and your client reaching out to the vendors asking the same questions, which can lead to confusion and frustration for all parties! If there are a lot of changes to be made with the vendors, it's best to have the client reach out first with the new information. You would then follow up with the vendors afterwards to ensure those changes have been made and match up with your information. If there is not much to change, then let the client know that you will be reaching out to their vendors and filling them in on any details that were decided on during the meeting. If your client hasn't already by this point, ask them to let their vendors know that they've hired a wedding coordinator and that they should expect to hear from you to discuss the plans! You'll also want to lay out your plans for working on their timeline. Let them know when you expect to have it completed (which is typically between one to two weeks ahead of the wedding day). Lastly, you'll want to confirm the date, time, and location of the rehearsal, and wrap up the meeting by reviewing any tasks you have given to them. They should leave the meeting with a clear sense of direction, but also with a sense of relief knowing that they are no longer on their own!

COMMUNICATING WITH VENDORS AND BUILDING THE TIMELINE

Now that you have an in-depth understanding of your client's wishes, your next step will be to contact each of your client's vendors to ensure their information matches yours! Whether you choose to reach out via phone or email, be mindful to come across as cooperative as opposed to controlling or demanding. Here is an example of how I begin my communications with vendors:

> *"Hello Mandy,*
> *My name is Allison and I am the wedding coordinator for Rachel and Jordan, (Uptown Market wedding on July 12th). I wanted to reach out and introduce myself as well as touch base on the plans for the day. I'm working on putting together a detailed timeline for their wedding day and I'd love to get your input!"*

From here, depending on which vendor you are contacting, you can include the basic timeline for the day and ask if that matches what they have as well. If it's the photographer you're contacting, ask if they have a photography timeline they could share with you, which could include estimated times for pre-ceremony photos, the first look, post-ceremony photos, any off-site photos (and locations), and/or golden hour photos. You can then confirm (or ask for) their arrival and departure times. Continue with any additional questions that you have that are specific to their services. Aside from confirming the "black and white" details, you'll want to get their input on timing. For example, ask the caterer how long he expects dinner service to take for the client's guest count, or ask the officiant how long she expects the ceremony to last. End the communication by asking if there are any questions you can answer for them, or if there is any additional information they still need from the client. More often than not, they will respond with a few questions of their own. Between yourself and the vendor, you'll be able to comb through the plans to ensure nothing has been overlooked!

There is no perfect order for reaching out to vendors. It heavily depends on what information you have, and what information you need. Oftentimes the photographer or DJ is a good starting point. They will both have a lot of involvement in the timing of the day and will have some good input. As you work your way through contacting each vendor, be sure to add any details that you've learned to the timeline. Perhaps the caterer let you know that the service staff will arrive at 3:30 p.m. to begin setting up for cocktail hour. Put it in the timeline! Maybe the rental company informed you that they will arrive at 11:00 p.m. to pick up the rentals. Put it in the timeline! The more information you have on the timeline, the more likely you are to identify any oversights, and the better your chances are of ensuring a smooth and successful wedding day for your clients!

"Just how important is this timeline anyway?" Good question! Suffice it to say, your chances of success are slim without it! Think of the timeline as your step-by-step wedding day manual! Every event, big or small, that will take place on the wedding day, should be included in the timeline. "So, what you're saying is, it should be thorough!" Absolutely! It should most definitely be thorough! You want anyone who reads it to have a clear-cut understanding of how the day will go. "Got it! So how do I create this magnificent document?" I'm so glad you asked! You start with the most important event of the whole day: the ceremony. By this point, your clients should already have a set ceremony start time. From here, you can work your way backwards to lay out the earlier pieces of the day. If it's feasible, try to include at least thirty minutes of down time immediately preceding the ceremony. This will give everyone a moment to relax and attend to any final touch-ups before the ceremony! This also serves as a little "cushion time" in the event that any pre-ceremony events are running behind.

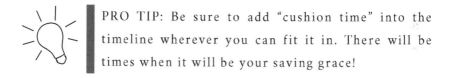

PRO TIP: Be sure to add "cushion time" into the timeline wherever you can fit it in. There will be times when it will be your saving grace!

Next, you'll want to factor in any pre-ceremony events that your client has planned. Did they want to do a first look? Were there any photos they wanted to get done before the ceremony? Were they going to read letters written to one another or exchange gifts? Are there any specific lunch plans or breakfast plans? All of these things need to have a designated spot on the timeline so you can be certain they get done! The day will move very quickly and some of these things could easily get forgotten in the hustle. By putting them on your timeline, you can make certain your clients get every memory they hoped for!

The next thing you'll want to factor in is any travel time. Will there be any driving from the getting ready location to the venue? Will anyone be meeting at an off-site location for photos? A common mistake couples make when laying out their timeline is failing to factor in "transition time," especially when it comes to travel time! For example, let's say the bride is expected to be done with hair and makeup at 2:00 p.m. and Google Maps says it takes fifteen minutes to get to the venue from the salon. So, she puts in her timeline that she will arrive at the venue at 2:15 p.m. She also has her photographer scheduled to meet her and her bridesmaids at the venue for some "getting ready" photos, which she was told would take about fifteen minutes. The photographer is then scheduled to meet with the groom and groomsmen for their pre-ceremony photos at 2:30 p.m. which is set to be done at 2:45 p.m., leaving "just enough time" to have a few minutes to relax before the 3:00 p.m. ceremony! Through a wedding coordinator's eyes, this is a hot mess! I can tell you that, at *best*, this ceremony will be starting a half hour late. Here's why. Let's say the bridal party does in fact get done with hair and makeup at their planned time of 2:00 p.m. They do not, at that very moment in time, immediately begin traveling towards the venue. They will likely still need to gather up all of their stuff, take a few selfies, handle payments, share their new look with each other, and enjoy the moment for a second! Once they do make their way to their mode of transportation, there's still the inevitable "just a minute, I have to go to the bathroom" or "hold on a second, I forgot my purse!" It's now 2:20 p.m. and they haven't even left the salon yet. You can see how it would go from there! In most cases, it is best to double the anticipated drive time to account for these real-life factors. At the very least, adding an extra ten minutes per trip will help to prevent going down that slippery slope of falling behind schedule!

Once you've worked out the pre-ceremony events and travel times, you will then know the time by which your clients will need to be done getting ready! Once you have that handy little piece of the puzzle, you can then use your math skills to figure out what time they should *begin* getting ready! Or if they already have a start time, then you can confirm whether or not their allotted getting ready time will be sufficient. This is where all of the information you gathered from the vendors will prove to be vital. Believe it or not, sometimes these things aren't so well thought out, and it will be up to you to find and point out any insufficiencies. From here you can fill in any remaining pre-ceremony plans, if any, and begin adding the nitty-gritty details!

- Add vendor arrival and setup or delivery times.
- Add your own arrival time and list any setup responsibilities you have.
- Include a list of items that should be complete upon your arrival so that you can be sure to check that they are done as soon as you get there!
- If anyone is going to be delivering any items to you (e.g. the couple has asked the groom's brother to drop off the printed menus to the venue), be sure to include this in your timeline as well.
- Include the time the venue opens for access.
- If the bride wants some special photos of her getting into her dress, you should assign a specific time for that as well to help ensure all parties are where they need to be, when they need to be there.

- Include relevant parties' arrival times (e.g. bride, groom, wedding party, parents, etc.).
- Any time-sensitive tasks you have should also be added to the timeline (e.g. a reminder to pin the boutonnieres onto the groom's and groomsmen's jackets before pre-ceremony pictures).
- Include a reminder to double check that all ceremony items are in place (candles, lighters, wine glasses, flower baskets, signs, etc.).
- Include the time any planned music should begin.
- If any vendors have mentioned tasks they have planned for specific times (e.g. the officiant wants to meet with the couple twenty minutes before the ceremony), go ahead and add those to the timeline as well.
- Include reminders to ensure anyone who was assigned a job is where they need to be at the right time (e.g. parking attendant, ushers, guestbook or wedding program attendants).
- Add the wedding party lineup time and location(s). Include a list of all wedding attendants' names in the order in which they will be lined up.
- Include all songs (as precisely as possible) that are to accompany any ceremony proceedings.
- Include a basic outline of the ceremony, from processional to recessional, and make a note of any announcements that the officiant should make immediately following the ceremony.

Most ceremonies (certainly not all, but most) will be thirty minutes long or less. If it's a simple, straight-forward ceremony with few or no "extras" (extras meaning readings, performances, or unity ceremonies), you may even be looking at a fifteen to twenty-minute ceremony. Add in a little extra time in the event that the ceremony gets delayed for any reason. Occasionally, you will have a wedding attendant on double (or even triple) duty. For example, maybe a groomsman has been asked to escort a special guest down the aisle and will then need to return to escort a bridesmaid down the aisle. Or maybe one of the bridesmaids has also been asked to officiate the ceremony! Keep these things in mind when working out the lineup order. On the sample timeline included in this book (see Appendix F), you will see an example of how I handle this type of situation to be as clear and non-confusing as possible!

Now you are ready to move on to the post-ceremony events. Typically, there will be a cocktail hour immediately following the ceremony. The length of cocktail hour depends on several factors; the most important factor being the couple's photography wishes. For example, if the couple will be doing a first look before the ceremony and only has a small list of group photos they would like taken during cocktail hour, then one hour will easily be sufficient. However, if they have chosen not to do a first look, or if they have a long list of group photos to be taken, then it may be necessary to add an additional thirty minutes to cocktail hour. Of course, if the venue is separate from the ceremony venue, be sure to include travel time! Include any tasks that will need to be done during cocktail hour (such as moving floral arrangements, lighting candles on the guests' dinner tables, or ensuring the couple signs the marriage license). Determine what time you'll want to have the guests begin getting seated. It's helpful to have the MC make this announcement. If the couple has chosen to partake in a grand entrance, you'll want to make note of the time and location for getting them lined up. To make it easy on yourself, list the names of everyone who will be introduced in the correct order on your timeline so you can get them lined up quickly and efficiently. List the time that the actual introductions will begin.

PRO TIP: When listing the names of the wedding attendants participating in the grand entrance on your timeline, include the exact verbiage by which each attendant will be introduced. You can also include the phonetic spelling of any tricky names, which will be handy when going over the plan with the MC!

There is a lot of variation in what happens next at a wedding reception, so how you proceed from here will depend on your client's preferences. Perhaps your client has chosen to go right into their first dance, or maybe they have decided to sit down for dinner first. Depending on your client's unique plans, some additional things you may need to include in the timeline are:

- Special dances (and accompanying songs)
- MC announcements or introductions (e.g. announcing the shuttle schedule or introducing the bride's grandfather for the blessing)
- Any speeches or toasts (including names and/or titles)
- Dinner service schedule (by course, if applicable)
- Any time-sensitive vendor tasks (e.g. bartenders pour champagne before toast or caterers slice cake after cake cutting)
- Any scheduled vendor breaks
- Any special events to occur during the reception (and accompanying songs)

- o   Bouquet or garter toss
- o   Anniversary dance
- o   Cake cutting
- o   Shoe game
- o   The Horah dance
- Any scheduled bar closings
- Any late-night food plans
- Vendor departure times
- Any special send-off plans
  - o   Sparkler exit
  - o   Glow sticks
  - o   Decorating of couple's car
- Cleanup plans (e.g. caterers pull linens or bartenders clear glasses)
- End of night responsibilities (e.g. Allison packs up décor or groom's parents take gifts and cards)
- Reminders to distribute final payments or tips, if applicable
- Venue close time

Once you have every last detail added to the timeline, you will then want to have the couple review it. This gives them a clear picture of how every moment of their day will transpire. Oftentimes, even though the client has made the majority of the decisions for their wedding day, it can still be difficult for them to put together all of the pieces and see the day as a whole. Reviewing the timeline will give them an opportunity to really get a feel for the flow of their day, and will allow them to more easily determine if any changes or adjustments will be needed. Do not worry! Any changes requested at this point are typically minor adjustments and should not require you to redo the entire timeline! Sometimes, a couple might want to simply move the bouquet toss up twenty minutes or push cake cutting back a little. Once you have a final version that has been approved by the clients, you will then want to share the timeline with all relevant vendors. Typically, this includes the photographer, videographer, catering team, bartenders, DJ or band, and the venue manager, if applicable. Vendors who will not be present for the entirety of the event (such as the florist, baker, hair and makeup artists, or rental company) typically won't need a copy of the timeline, as a good majority of the information on it will be of little relevance to them. As long as you've confirmed the details of their services, they should be good to go! One thing to be aware of is that vendors often have a set way of doing things, and just because you've shared your very detailed and well-thought-out timeline with them, doesn't mean they are going to use it (or even look at it)! Sometimes vendors prefer to use their own timeline. It's part of their normal routine and trying to follow a completely different format might throw them off their game. Inevitably, this can give rise to inconsistencies. This can happen in a number of ways. Sometimes, a couple will make a change and inform their vendor, but forget to share that information with you as well. Sometimes, you inform the vendor of a change, and they simply forget to update their timeline. By reviewing upcoming events with each vendor throughout the day, you will hopefully be able to catch any of these discrepancies before any mistakes happen!

THE REHEARSAL

As the wedding coordinator, your next task is to facilitate the rehearsal. Typically, the wedding rehearsal is held the evening before the wedding, but for various reasons, this is not always the case. Some venues will be booked for another event the night before your client's wedding and may require rehearsals to be done in the middle of the week. Oftentimes, this can prove to be quite difficult for couples and their wedding parties, especially if they are from out of town. For this reason, it may be necessary to conduct a rehearsal at an off-site location. I have done rehearsals in backyards, parks, basketball courts, and even once in the lobby of a hotel! As long as *you* know the layout of the ceremony space and can help the wedding party visualize it as you take them through the steps, you can make it work!

Prior to the rehearsal, you'll want to get yourself organized by putting together a rehearsal outline (see Appendix G). This will help you with all of the wedding attendants' names and placements, as well as keep you on track throughout the rehearsal. Much of this can be copied right from your timeline!

Upon your arrival at the rehearsal site, take some time to meet with the officiant to discuss each of your roles and responsibilities for the day, as well as the overall plan for executing the rehearsal. Some officiants prefer to take the lead in running the rehearsal, while others may have little to no experience and will need you to take charge! Just as with any other vendor, you will come across personalities of all kinds! Some will respect your position and appreciate your help, others not so much. Do your best to avoid generating any tension between yourself and the officiant, unless, of course, you absolutely have to for the sake of the client. If an officiant expresses a desire to facilitate the rehearsal, I have no problem taking a step back and letting them take the lead. After all, they are the ones who will be front and center during the actual ceremony! In this scenario, I simply help with lineup and offer any additional support where needed. Again, most officiants will be happy to work in tandem with you at the rehearsal, but if you're sensing a little pushback, it's best to take a back seat on this one!

In addition to meeting with the officiant, you should also meet with anyone else who has a special role during the ceremony (e.g. readers, performers, ushers, or other attendants) to ensure they fully understand their role, including start times, locations, and any special instructions. If they are not in attendance at the rehearsal, make a point to touch base with them before the ceremony on the wedding day.

As many experienced wedding coordinators have learned, there is a preferred order for running through the rehearsal, and it's not necessarily in sequence. Instead of beginning with the processional, it is best to start in the middle and practice a few steps individually before putting it all together! Below is my standard rehearsal process:

- Introductions/overview
- Line up the wedding party for the ceremony
- Practice the recessional
- Practice the processional
- Review the ceremony
- Complete run-through

INTRODUCTIONS/OVERVIEW. Introduce yourself and give a brief run-through of how the rehearsal will go. Letting the attendants know ahead of time what to expect will eliminate a lot of confusion and questions from the wedding party which can disrupt the flow of the rehearsal and extend the time it takes to get through it.

LINE UP THE WEDDING PARTY FOR THE CEREMONY. Start by having the wedding party line up in the places in which they will stand during the ceremony. This will help to ensure a smooth transition once you begin practicing the processional. When the attendants already know where to go after walking in, you won't have to stop in the middle of the processional to help them get to their designated spots. This will allow for a much more seamless run-through!

PRACTICE THE RECESSIONAL. From here, you'll want to practice walking out. Begin by instructing the bride to retrieve her bouquet from the maid of honor (even if it's just an "air bouquet," still have her practice). Next, have the bride take the groom's arm and begin walking down the aisle. For a little fun, encourage the rehearsal attendants to cheer and shout for the couple! This always puts a smile on their faces! Allow the couple to make their way completely down the aisle before instructing the next pair to begin their exit. Instruct the following couples to wait until the pair ahead of them gets halfway down the aisle before heading down. If the couple has chosen to include their parents or other special guests in the recessional, ask the officiant to help facilitate this. Have him or her walk up to where the special guests are seated and signal for them to exit. Typically, the bride's parents will be the first to exit, followed by the groom's parents.

PRACTICE THE PROCESSIONAL. Now that you have the ceremony placement and recessional nailed down, it's time to practice the processional! Take a moment to gather everyone involved in the processional to go over the plan. Explain where everyone will be lining up, who will go first, second, and third, and what their cue will be to begin walking. Give them a few aisle-walking tips (ladies on the left, walk at a pace slightly slower than a comfortable stroll, bouquets held around the hip area, etc.). Once you've covered the game plan, you can then work on getting everyone lined up! Sometimes, this means getting different groups lined up in several different locations around the venue. For example, you may have the officiant and groom lined up close to the altar, the special guests lined up near the aisle entrance, the wedding party lined up in the hallway, and the bride and her escort hiding away in the next room! This can take a few minutes to organize, but getting everyone familiar with their lineup spots will definitely help things run more smoothly on the wedding day!

Once you have everyone in their places, cue the first group to begin walking. Be sure to let them know how to space themselves out. Try to point out a landmark or "halfway point" for them to allow the couple ahead to reach before beginning to walk. Don't be afraid to step in and give a little guidance if things aren't looking quite right.

Continue to cue each group. If there are any children in the processional, be sure to help them feel as comfortable as possible and let them know who to look for if they begin to feel nervous! Always have someone designated to help out in case any little ones get "frozen feet"!

Determine ahead of time if the officiant will be asking the guests to stand before the bride's entrance. Some officiants feel this is an unnecessary step, as people will often do it on their own when they see the bride. Personally, I think it looks better when the guests all rise together and are already standing when the bride makes her entrance, as opposed to everyone popping up out of their seats once they realize she's already coming. Either way, be sure to know the officiant's plan so you can include this in the rehearsal.

Getting the bride down the aisle is one feat; a smooth hand-off is an accomplishment all on its own! This can be an incredibly awkward moment in an otherwise seamless ceremony if not practiced ahead of time. Will the father kiss the bride on the cheek? Will he shake the groom's hand or give him a hug? Will the officiant have some words to say before the father takes his seat? It may feel a little silly, but all of these things need to be practiced!

PROCESSIONAL TIPS:

- For the seating of the special guests, have the second pair entering the beginning of the aisle as the first pair is just getting to their seats
- Have the wedding party space out about half an aisle length (more for a short aisle or less for a longer aisle)
- For a large wedding party, shorten the spacing in between pairs to ensure everyone makes it down the aisle before the song ends
- For anyone with double duty, have them walk around the outside of the ceremony seating when returning to the lineup, instead of directly back down the aisle
- Instruct the attendants to walk at a casual pace
- Bouquets should be held low, around the hip area, not up by the chest
- Once the bride reaches the altar, she should hand her bouquet over to the Maid of Honor
- If the bride's dress has a long train, instruct the Maid of Honor to straighten it out once the bride is in her position at the altar

REVIEW THE CEREMONY. Next, you will want to review the ceremony. Ask the officiant to go over the main components of the ceremony so that everyone knows what to expect. Practice anything that involves a change of positioning or an exchange of something. Will the officiant have the couple face the guests at any point? Practicing this will help them get their footing down and spacing worked out. Will there be a reader? Practice having the officiant invite them up. What path will they take? Will the bride and groom step off to the side? As a general rule, nobody should walk between the bride and groom during the ceremony (it's symbolic), so practicing these transitions will help to avoid any wedding day faux pas. Discuss how the couple should stand during the majority of the ceremony. Will they face each other or face the officiant? Will they hold hands? If so, one or two hands? Remember, you are aiming for a seamless ceremony on the wedding day. Each of these seemingly small details can turn into fumbles if not planned out in advance! If the couple has planned a unity ceremony, practice this in detail. Depending on where the unity ceremony will take place, this may involve having half of the wedding party change positions. You definitely want to work out any kinks with that transition!

As the officiant concludes the ceremony review, be sure to take note of his or her final statement. Oftentimes this is the introduction of the couple, but not always. You'll want to know this information to share with the DJ or musician, as it will be their cue to begin the recessional song.

COMPLETE RUN-THROUGH. Now it's time to put all of the pieces together! Have all attendants reconvene at their meeting spots and get lined up. Cue the first group to begin and stay nearby to help with spacing. Do this with each group, just as you did the first time, except this time it should go much more smoothly! Once the bride and her escort have made their way down the aisle, have them go through the motions of the hand-off one last time. Quickly review the ceremony and rehearse any transitions or exchanges once more. Review any cues the officiant will give to the ceremony participants when it is time for their part. Run through the recessional one final time, reminding the wedding party to fill in the gap as couples ahead of them pair up and exit. Also, review the spacing and when they should begin walking. Once the entire wedding party, and any special guests involved in the recessional, have made their way down the aisle, review with the officiant any announcements he or she should make at this point. If there will be ushers or anyone else dismissing the guests after the ceremony, you can do a quick run-through with them at this time. Instruct them to start with the front row on the bride's side and alternate sides as they move down the aisle. Utilizing two ushers is ideal, but it can be done with one. If the couple has not made plans for anyone to dismiss the guests, I would highly recommend having the officiant make an announcement to give the guests some instruction so they are not left wondering what they should be doing.

That's it! As long as everyone feels comfortable with their roles, and the bride and groom give their nod of approval, you can call it a wrap! Be sure to thank everyone for their time and effort. Review arrival times for the wedding day, particularly for the bride, groom, and wedding party, and go over any relevant transportation information. Remind the bride and groom of important items they should not forget to bring on the wedding day, such as the rings, marriage license, vows, or other essential items. Ensure everyone's questions have been answered and send them off to the rehearsal dinner!

PRO TIP: If, during the rehearsal, any minor changes were made or new information was brought to light, be sure to update your timeline as soon as possible and inform any relevant vendors.

Oftentimes, you will be invited by the couple to join them at the rehearsal dinner. It will be up to you to determine your own policy on this, but, as a coordinator, it is not necessary for you to attend. Traditionally, the rehearsal dinner is a more intimate affair with close family and friends, so being there with a bunch of people you don't know, and who don't know you, could feel a little awkward. You could also find yourself in an uncomfortable situation considering the ones who have invited you are typically not the ones who are footing the bill! Instead, spend this time working on any final preparations for the wedding day and getting some good rest!

MANAGING THE WEDDING DAY

The big day has finally arrived! You are well rested, fully caffeinated, your timeline is flawless, and you are ready to conquer the day! Before you walk out that door, be sure you have the following items to help get you through the day:

- WEDDING DAY SURVIVAL KIT. When putting together your wedding day survival kit, try to imagine every little thing that could go wrong. Scary, I know, but effective! Now make a list of every item you can think of (at least every portable item) that could help to remedy each of the problems you envisioned. Here's a list of some basics to get you started!

- Safety pins
- Corsage pins
- Sewing kit
- Eye drops
- Floss sticks
- Deodorant
- Disposable razor
- Breath mints
- Batteries
- Scissors
- Tape
- Fashion tape
- Wire cutters
- Floral wire
- First-aid kit
- Hair pins
- Earring backs
- Baby wipes
- Hand sanitizer
- Clear nail polish
- Hair spray
- Concealer stick
- Tissues
- Tweezers
- Nail clippers
- Needle-nose plyers
- Tide pen
- Lint roller

- Pens
- Permanent markers
- Twine
- White ribbon
- Candle lighters
- Peanut-free granola bars
- Water

When it comes to packing all of these items, your best bet (and a favorite among wedding coordinators and planners) is a rolling makeup case, which, unsurprisingly, is exactly what makeup artists use! It has several different compartments and is easy to transport, so you can keep your items organized and easily accessible.

- CLIPBOARD OR TABLET. If you're going the traditional paper route with your documents, opt for a clipboard that is part folder (aka the clipboard-folio)! You'll keep the timeline readily accessible on the outside, and other relevant documents you may need quick access to on the inside. Typically, these would include the seating assignment list, floor plan, décor instructions, and a list of items being delivered, if applicable. Also, if you've been tasked with handing out any vendor payments or tips, you will have a safe place to hold them!

  If you are more comfortable going digital, a tablet makes a great alternative option! You'll have quick and easy access to *all* of your documents without all of the inevitable paper shuffling! If you're going this route, just be sure you have a way to access the documents offline. In addition, it might be wise to have a backup plan in the case of a complete device malfunction! Whether it's printed copies or a backup tablet, having a plan B ensures you don't find yourself in an awful predicament!

- SNACKS. Do yourself a huge favor and don't forget the snacks! While eating may be the furthest thing from your mind, it is far from the least important! Remember that wedding hangover you learned about earlier? You want to avoid that as much as possible, and taking care of your basic human needs is a pretty good start! And, at the risk of sounding like a well-meaning but slightly overbearing mother, don't forget your water!

- RENTALS. Perhaps you've accumulated a collection of cake stands or an assortment of card boxes that you have decided to rent out to needing clients! While this may not be the most profound piece of advice you've ever been given, don't forget to bring it! Make a note right at the top of your timeline, or tie a string around your finger. Whatever it takes to ensure that any items you have agreed to bring don't get left behind!

- CONTRACTS. In addition to the timeline and other important documents, you should also be sure to bring your folder containing all vendor contracts. You don't necessarily need to carry them around with you all day long, but having them available to access, if the situation calls for it, is highly advantageous. Also, bringing an extra copy or two of the timeline is always a good idea!

- A WATCH. This one doesn't need much explanation. You need a watch. I will say that if your watch is also a fitness tracker, it is very interesting to learn how many steps you take on wedding days! Here's a hint: it's a lot!

On the day of the wedding, plan to arrive at least fifteen minutes early. This allows for any traffic occurrences, or at the very least, a few minutes to review the timeline once more. Take advantage of any spare time you have to focus and relax, because more often than not, the second you arrive on scene, you will be needed (assuming your phone hasn't already blown up)!

Upon your arrival, check in with the clients if they are on-site. Ensure all is well and things are on track (they likely will have started getting ready well before you arrive). Check on all items that should be completed at this point. Is the room layout correct? Are the table and chair counts accurate? If each table is set to have a specific and varying number of seats, oftentimes this is where you'll find an error. For example, if Table 2 should have eight chairs, Table 3 should have nine chairs, and Tables 4 and 5 should have ten chairs, you want to make sure the counts are accurate. If overlooked, this can become quite a mess when the guests begin to arrive! Are the linens set? Do the place settings look correct? If any rentals have been delivered, is everything accounted for? Once you've ensured things are up to par, begin any décor setup you are responsible for. Your time is gold; you'll want to use it wisely! Start by focusing on the more time-consuming tasks (e.g. laying out place cards or wedding favors). The later it gets, the more likely you are to face interruptions. The quicker tasks will be easier to accomplish between the many other things you will be called on to handle as the day progresses.

As vendors begin to arrive, be sure to greet them. Be available to answer any questions they may have, but avoid being intrusive. Allow them some time to get oriented and set up before you begin an in-depth review of the plans. It is during this time of the day you will most often find yourself being pulled in many directions. You may be in the middle of placing the table numbers when the maid of honor asks for your help looking for the gold markers they brought for the guestbook. During your search, the catering manager comes over to request your assistance with deciding where the dessert table should be placed, because the original placement blocks the servers' path to the patio. While you are addressing this, the florist asks for a moment of your time to go over how to remove the arrangement he just hung on the arbor, since he won't be there to do it at the end of the night. You are then approached by the DJ who informs you that he doesn't have enough outlets and needs a power strip in order to operate all of his equipment! Knowing how to prioritize your everchanging task list (and staying calm no matter how stressed you feel) is vitally important. Cross things off on your timeline as they get accomplished. This will help you to easily see what is next to do, and will help to keep you more aware of the time!

PRO TIP: When the tasks begin to pile up, it is helpful to keep notes on your timeline of any jobs left unfinished, so you can be sure to come back to them when you have time!

Check in with vendors several times throughout the day. Keep them informed of the day's progress, especially if things are ahead of or behind schedule. Seemingly minor adjustments in the timing of the day can make a big difference for certain vendors, particularly the caterers! If you're running fifteen minutes behind and haven't given them notice, that could severely impact the quality of the food they serve, and not in a good way!

Keeping everyone in the loop and on the same page helps to ensure the day moves forward as smoothly as possible.

Keep your timeline with you at all times! Your job is to keep the day on track, and in order to do that, you need to be two steps ahead of everyone else! If an event is coming up, you need to be sure all key players are in place, and everyone has what they need for that event to begin on time. For example, if the wedding party is doing pre-ceremony photos at 1:00 p.m., you need to be sure the ladies all have their bouquets, and the guys all have their boutonnieres secured to their jackets by 12:50 p.m. Then, see that they have all attended to any final adjustments or touchups, and are at the designated location, along with the photographer, by the starting time.

As the ceremony time nears, be sure to touch base with all relevant vendors to briefly review the plan. Discuss the order of events, timing, cues, and specific song selections to ensure accuracy across all vendors. Check to see that all ceremony items are in place. Is the décor complete? Are the rings in the ring box? Do the flower girls have their baskets and petals? Are the unity ceremony items in place? If any microphones are being used, it may be a good idea to have the DJ (or sound person) meet with whomever will be using one to be certain they are comfortable operating it. If there are any readers or performers, touch base with them to see that they have everything they need for their part. It's also a good idea to provide the officiant with extra copies of any readings or vows (if the couple has written their own).

Just before you line up the wedding party, see to it that all of the guests have made their way to the ceremony site. Once the guests have cleared the area, line the wedding party up just as you did at the rehearsal. Keep an eye out for any guests who may still be arriving (aka the stragglers)! When the coast is clear, cue the music! Once you have the ceremony in motion, stay nearby to make sure everything goes as planned.

After the ceremony, help transition everyone to the next event. Typically, this means photos for the wedding party and cocktail hour for the guests. See to it that everyone gets to where they need to be! Check in with all cocktail hour vendors to ensure things are moving along according to schedule. Oftentimes you will have some things to accomplish during this time, such as moving décor pieces or lighting candles. Once you've completed your tasks, touch base with each vendor to discuss the upcoming events.

When checking in with the DJ, band, or MC, be sure to discuss the following:

- GRAND INTRODUCTIONS
  - Where will they take place?
  - Where will you have the wedding party line up?
  - Do you both have the same order and list of names?
  - Do you both have the same song selections listed for the introductions?
  - Are there any tricky names to review?

- SPEECHES AND TOASTS
  - Who will be giving a speech or toast and when?
  - Will the MC bring the microphone to them, or have them come up to the front to give their speech?
  - Will the MC introduce each person, or have the guests hand off the microphone themselves to the next person speaking?

- CAKE CUTTING
    - When will this happen?
    - Where will this take place?
    - Did the couple pick a specific song for this?

- SPECIAL DANCES
    - When will the first dance take place?
    - When will other special dances take place?
    - Do you both have the same songs listed for these?

- OTHER RECEPTION EVENTS (IF ANY)
    - When will they take place and where?
    - Are there any special items that will be needed for the event (for example, two chairs for the shoe game)?

- ANNOUNCEMENTS
    - Will the MC need to make any announcements? If so, what and when?

PRO TIP: For any guests who will have a speaking role during the reception, locate and make note of where they will be seated. This is great information to share with the MC and will help him or her to facilitate the speeches flawlessly!

After you've worked out all of the details with the DJ, band, or MC, connect with the catering manager to ensure they are up to speed on the plan as well. Will the toasts take place before the food is served, after it is served, or in between courses? If the dinner is buffet style, who will be releasing the tables? Are there any special instructions or requests they should know about? Check in with the bartenders as well. Are they pouring champagne for the guests before the toasts? Will they be closing for any period of time? Staying on top of communication with the vendors is one of the most important jobs you have on the wedding day! Even if it feels redundant, you should always communicate with the vendors about upcoming events. It can mean the difference between a seamless day and one that completely falls apart!

As the end of cocktail hour nears, connect with any guests who will have a speaking role during the reception. Believe it or not, I have had guests who were unaware that they were supposed to be giving a speech (or toast, or blessing)! By checking in with them ahead of time, you can be certain they will be prepared when their time comes.

Once cocktail hour ends, you'll need to ensure all of the guests get seated at their tables. Sounds simple enough, but that's not always the case! More often than not, when the MC makes the announcement for guests to find their seats, a good chunk of them will head to the bar! Waiting for these guests to get their drinks can cause quite a delay in the schedule, and no matter how many times you, or the MC, asks them to sit, most will not budge! I've had guests get pretty testy with me in this situation and it can get uncomfortable very quickly. It's best to avoid the situation as much as possible by giving the guests a fifteen-minute heads up before the end of cocktail hour. You will still have those who will wait until the end, but this way you'll at least minimize that last-minute rush to the bar. As an additional measure, you can also plan to have the bartenders close down the bar at a set time. If asking politely doesn't work, a closed bar will certainly do the trick!

If the couple has chosen to do a grand entrance, plan on getting everyone lined up about ten minutes ahead of the scheduled introduction time. Sometimes, depending upon the nature of the group, this can be a little more challenging than you would think! This is often the first time, in a very busy and regimented day, that the wedding party gets to relax a little and have some fun! The last thing they want to do at this point is stand in another line, and participate in another formal event. Alas, the heckling begins! You know the type! They've had a few drinks and they're trying to give you a hard time. Most of the time, it's all in good fun, but every so often you'll get a needler who takes it just a little too far. Do you know what hecklers hate the most? To be ignored! And that is your secret weapon. Stay focused on just doing your job. You'll usually have some sympathetic helpers within the group who will step in if another member of the wedding party is getting too far out of line (both figuratively and literally)! It can also be helpful (and mutually beneficial) to ask the MC to assist you in this endeavor. They can help you get the attention of an unruly group, and also, if needed, review the names of the wedding party members, since they will be the one doing the introductions.

Do your best to ensure that dinner service rolls out smoothly. Unfortunately, this is one of those areas that you have very little control over, and if there ends up being a delay in the schedule, this is usually where it will happen. Don't get me wrong, what caterers can pull off is nothing short of magic! Feeding 150+ people is no easy feat! With that being said, mistakes happen! Just as they do with all of us at one point or another. If dinner service is falling behind, stay on top of your job by keeping the lines of communication open between yourself and the catering team, and also between yourself and the couple! Keeping your clients in the loop (when necessary) can help alleviate any tension or frustration they may feel when things aren't going according to plan! Additionally, while you may feel obligated to hastily remedy the situation, resist the urge to hound the caterers. I guarantee they are feeling the pressure and are doing everything they can to get back on track. It's completely appropriate to request a status update or two, but losing your cool, or excessively "checking in," would be counterproductive. Short of jumping in the kitchen and putting plates together yourself (not recommended), there is not much you can do at this point but wait. Sometimes you can recruit the DJ (or band) for a little assistance in keeping the room entertained if things are really delayed. Otherwise, stay calm, keep everyone informed, get creative, and roll with the punches!

Don't forget to eat! You, along with all the other vendors, should take a few moments to sit down and eat dinner! Some vendors will have strict policies on this (like where they sit, what they eat, and how much time they are allotted). Others will be much more flexible. Regardless of your preferences, it is important to take a break when there is a little down time. Wedding days are very long and hard on your body, so taking a moment to recharge and fuel up is crucial!

As dinner comes to an end, start getting prepped for the next event. For some, this will be the traditional cutting of the cake! First, you'll want to consult with the photographer. They should have some input on how best to tackle this, taking into account lighting, angles, the background, etc. Next, make sure the cake knife and server are on the table. Grab a small plate from the caterers, along with a few napkins, and set those on the table as well. When you have everything ready, grab the couple. Give them a quick tutorial on how to cut the cake. Instruct them to grab the knife and together make two cuts (to form a triangular piece) in the bottom tier. Then, using the server, slide the piece onto the plate and cut it in half. They can use their hands to each pick up a half and feed it to each other. Whatever they decide to do from there is on them! When the couple is ready, have the MC make an announcement, and be sure the photographer (and videographer, if applicable) are ready. Once the announcement is made, the couple will take it from there!

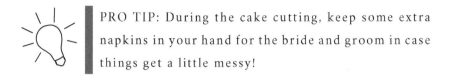

PRO TIP: During the cake cutting, keep some extra napkins in your hand for the bride and groom in case things get a little messy!

A large part of the remainder of your evening will be spent hunting people down! A task that, as you will soon learn, gets more difficult as the night goes on! Imagine the bride and groom have just finished their first dance. The groom walks off the floor as the MC invites the father of the bride up to dance with his daughter, but Dad doesn't come. Turns out, he's in the bathroom! Kind of takes the wind out of the sail of that special moment, doesn't it? This is a potentially embarrassing situation that is best to avoid entirely. For any special dances, or other special reception events, be sure to give participants a five to ten-minute warning, and then be sure you have eyes on them before you give the MC the OK! As always, make sure all key players are ready, and any needed items have been gathered as well.

Now that you've successfully managed the day's events, it's time to start prepping for the end of the night. Will anyone be decorating the bride and groom's getaway car? If so, see to it that this gets done! Start connecting with anyone who has been tasked with taking items home for the couple (such as gifts, cards, and décor), and discuss the plan. Has the couple planned any kind of grand exit (e.g. sparklers, bubbles, bells, etc.)? If so, gather the necessary items and place them by the area where they will be used. As the end of the reception nears, begin collecting smaller décor pieces. You don't want to strip the tables completely, as this will give the impression that the night is over before it's actually over.

However, given that you're typically working within a tight cleanup window, gathering the smaller pieces now will help to ensure you get everything (and everyone) out by the venue's closing time!

If your policy includes staying through the end of the night, you'll want to see that cleanup occurs swiftly and efficiently. We all know the phrase "what goes up must come down," but something that clients often don't think about is that what goes *in* must come *out!* Too often I have seen people overwhelmed by the amount of stuff there is to take home at the end of the night and struggle to fit it all in their vehicle. Make it a point ahead of time to recommend that your clients designate at least two friends or family members (with two separate vehicles) to help transport the items at the end of the night.

If you've been asked to distribute any tips or final payments, make sure you do so before the vendors have left! Not all vendors will stay for the entirety of the event, so catching them before they head out will save you the hassle of dealing with this in the following days. Ensure vendors have fulfilled all of their duties when it comes to cleanup (e.g. bartenders have cleared all glassware, caterers have taken out the trash, etc.). You definitely don't want to be stuck with any additional tasks at the end of the night! Once all of the necessary items have been removed, the vendors have wrapped up, and the venue has been returned to its original condition, it is time to say goodbye! Be sure to congratulate the newlyweds and, if the mood strikes you, give them a big ole hug! The couple will likely express their gratitude for all of your help and *may* even offer you a tip!

As a nice gesture, I recommend adding a small personal touch to your services! You can leave a small gift for the couple, or simply a card with a heartfelt message! Just a little something to let them know you appreciate them for entrusting the most important day of their lives to you! After a day or two, you may also send them a follow-up email to, again, congratulate them and thank them for choosing you. This is also a good opportunity to ask them to share their experience of working with you in a review! Be sure to include direct links to your profiles to make it as simple for them as possible. Don't worry if you don't hear back right away, most will be off on their honeymoon or busy with all of the post-wedding adjustments! While not all couples will follow through on their promise to write a review, you will find that most will, and it is an incredible feeling when you get that first five-star review! Truthfully, each one after that feels just as good too!

In the days following the wedding, you'll want to spend some time reflecting on your performance. Were there things you could have done differently? Ways in which you could have been better prepared? Things you may have overlooked ahead of the wedding day? Keep a list of notes for yourself on ways to improve your services, and ensure any mistakes are not repeated. If you found any of your current policies to be problematic, consider some alternative options. By continuously evaluating your services and your performance, you can be certain that you are doing the very best for your clients, as well as for your business!

Now that you've learned the basic steps for working with clients, you can start thinking about how you'll want to design your services. After some time and experience, you'll have a better understanding of what works best for you and your clients. With a basic service plan in place, you can then focus on setting up your business!

THREE

Starting Your Business

YOU NOW HAVE THE KNOWLEDGE to successfully manage a wedding day from beginning to end! You know how to conduct a client meeting and how to review vendor contracts. You know how to prep the ceremony site and how to keep the reception events on track. And you know how to put together a realistic timeline. In this Chapter, we will focus on the steps needed to get your business up and running! You will learn all the basics of starting a business, from brand development to pricing your service. With your business properly set up, you will be free to focus your attention on what matters most: your clients!

BUILD YOUR BRAND

The first thing you'll want to do is establish your brand. Think of your brand as the personality of your business. What image do you want your business to portray? What type of feeling do you want people to get when they interact with your business? Every aspect of your business should be a reflection of your brand. The name of your business, your website design, your logo, your business cards, even your own personal style should all be an extension of your brand. Building your brand takes a lot of thought and consideration, because once it's established, it can be difficult to change. Start by writing down a list of words that represent the style (or vibe) you are going for. For me, this list included words like unique, nontraditional, bold, creative, and colorful. Next, create a mood board by collecting images that appeal to you. They do not have to be wedding-specific images; you can draw inspiration from anywhere! In fact, I once used a coffee mug as inspiration for a color scheme! Head to the nearest home improvement store and grab some color samples to help you nail down your brand's color palette! Once you have a solid direction for your brand, you can then focus on developing each individual component.

NAME YOUR BUSINESS. When it comes to naming your business, there are several things to consider. First and foremost, does the name reflect your brand? Does it have a ring to it? Is it easy to pronounce? Does it sound good when said aloud? Additionally, you'll want to ensure the name is not already in use by another business and that it does not closely resemble the name of another established business (e.g. the Victoria's Secret/Victor's Secret debacle). Visit your state government's website to locate a database for searching registered business names to ensure your chosen business name is available. In addition, you'll want to visit the U.S Patent and Trademark Office's website to search nationwide for business names that have been trademarked (like Victoria's Secret) to ensure you don't run into any form of trademark infringement!

DEVELOP YOUR LOGO. Once you have decided on a business name, you'll then want to focus on developing your logo! Along with your business name, your logo is often where potential clients will get their first impression of your brand, so you'll want to make sure your logo lives up to its responsibility! Connect with an experienced graphic designer whose work befits your brand. Be sure to bring along your mood board to help your graphic designer get a sense of the style and direction you are going for.

PRO TIP: When developing your logo, be sure to have your graphic designer create a sub logo for you as well. A sub logo is essentially a condensed version of your main logo to use for smaller applications, such as social media profiles.

CREATE YOUR WEBSITE. One of your most important marketing tools will be your website! An impressionable website is often the deciding factor on whether or not a potential client hits that "contact" button! When it comes to building your website, you have two options. You can either do it yourself using a website building platform (such as Weebly, Wix, or Squarespace, to name a few) or opt to hire a web designer to build the website for you! The option you choose will largely depend on your budget, your tech-savviness, and your website needs. You may also want to have your graphic designer create some on-brand imagery for you to incorporate throughout your website. At the very least, you'll want a "Home" page that introduces viewers to your business, an "About" page where the viewer can learn more about you and your services, and a "Contact" page that gives the potential client a way to connect with you.

GET A BUSINESS PHONE NUMBER AND EMAIL ADDRESS. While it might be tempting to use your personal phone number, it is best to have a separate number for your business. It will give your business a stronger identity as well as a more professional look. You can simply get a second phone to use for your business, or opt to use a VoIP (Voice over IP) service. With VoIP service, you can get a separate business phone number without having to purchase a separate phone. Since calls are transmitted over the internet, you can use several different devices to make and receive calls using your business phone number. You would just need to have high-speed internet and an account with a VoIP service provider.

In addition to a separate business phone number, you should also secure a separate business email address. Not only does this help to keep your business more organized, but it also helps to show potential clients that you are a professional. Anyone can create a website and try to sell a service, but those that take the extra steps to formalize every aspect of their business tend to be viewed as more trustworthy, and thus more appealing to potential clients.

GET SOME BUSINESS CARDS. Business cards are a helpful tool when it comes to networking and growing your business. They are great to exchange with other vendors when building your referral network and also for handing out to potential clients! In addition, you can check with local wedding vendors who have physical stores (like bakeries, rental companies, dress boutiques, etc.) to see if they would allow you to leave a stack of your business cards on their counter or near their register. There are several great websites that make it easy to create your own business cards (such as www.vistaprint.com, www.canva.com, or www.got print.com). Just make sure you are being consistent with your brand!

CREATE YOUR SOCIAL MEDIA PAGES. It's almost a guarantee that anyone interested in your services is going to head straight for your social media pages! A strong social media presence gives greater credibility to your business, and gives the potential client a better feel for your personality and style. It can be difficult at first to come up with content for your social media pages. Start out by introducing yourself and a share a little bit about your business. Offer bits of advice for couples, or share the latest wedding trends. Share some images that inspire you! The earlier you start building your followers, the better! And once you have a few weddings under your belt, you'll have plenty to share!

PRO TIP: Always give credit to the photographer when sharing images on social media! It is, after all, their work you are using to promote your business; it's proper to return the favor!

GET HEADSHOTS. Another important step in the professionalization of your business is getting some high-quality headshots. Headshots help the viewer connect more with your business by giving them a little glimpse of the personality *behind* the business! A warm smile and a professional appearance will go a long way in setting a great first impression. I highly recommend having them done professionally! It is well worth the investment.

PLAN A STYLED SHOOT. A great way to get some on-brand imagery and showcase your design talents is to coordinate a styled wedding shoot. A styled shoot is essentially a mock wedding for the purpose of creating images that demonstrate each vendor's talents and skills. It involves coordinating a team of wedding vendors in a collaborative effort to bring to life a specific design concept. The images gained from the styled shoot are shared among all participating vendors where they may be used for marketing purposes. The images can also be submitted to various wedding blogs with the hopes of getting published, which is a great way to get your name out there and generate some business for all those involved! Once published, most blogs will send you a "badge" to share on your website to show that you've contributed to their blog. It's a great selling point for potential clients!

Depending upon the scale of your styled shoot, your costs may be minimal or substantial. Most vendors will offer their products and/or services without charge in exchange for the images. Some vendors, however, will require a minimal fee (for example, a delivery or setup fee for rented items). In order to pull off a specific look, you may need to purchase items if you cannot find them available to rent. I suggest creating a budget before you get started to ensure you don't get in over your head financially. You can really do a lot with a little, so don't feel like you need to break the bank on this. Use what you can from your vendors and make a few select purchases for a truly unique look. Then, let the photographer do what they do best! The hardest part will be waiting patiently for the images to be done with editing and delivered to your inbox, but I promise it will be worth the wait! See Appendix H for a list of steps on organizing a styled shoot.

MAKE IT LEGIT

Before you start operating your business, you'll need to go through some legal formalities to ensure your business is compliant with federal and state laws. Legitimizing your business is important for several reasons. It can provide you with some personal liability protection, improve your chances of securing a business loan, and can qualify you for certain tax benefits. And what's more, it will drastically increase your credibility in the eyes of potential clients! By following these simple steps, you'll be (legally) up and running in no time!

PRO TIP: Each state has its own set of rules and regulations for starting and operating a small business. Be sure to check your state's laws to ensure you complete all of the proper steps.

CHOOSE A BUSINESS STRUCTURE. You'll need to put some thought into how you want to structure your business. The business structure you choose will determine the taxes you will need to pay, the records you will be required to keep, and whether or not you are personally liable for your business's financial obligations. The most common business structures are the sole proprietorship, partnership, limited liability company, and corporation. Each structure has its own pros and cons, and its own set of benefits, requirements, and costs. Consult with a CPA to determine which structure makes the most sense for your business.

APPLY FOR AN EMPLOYER IDENTIFICATION NUMBER. An Employer Identification Number (EIN) is essentially a social security number for your business. It is issued by the IRS in order to keep track of your business's tax reporting. You can apply easily by visiting www.irs.gov. You'll need to wait until after your business structure has been formed, and any related applications have been approved, before applying for your EIN.

REGISTER YOUR BUSINESS NAME. It's important to register your business name in order to prevent any other business from using the same name! It also allows you to legally conduct business under a name other than your own. If, for example, a client decides to pay with a check, and they make it out to your business name, you won't be allowed to cash that check unless your business name is registered. In addition, opening a business bank account requires that you have a registered business name. Check with your state and local governments to determine how to register a business name in your area.

GET LIABILITY INSURANCE. As a small business owner who works directly with clients, you'll need to carry liability insurance. Let's say you are helping affix some decorations to the arbor when it suddenly begins to tip. If the arbor falls and breaks, your insurance could cover the cost to replace it. Or worse, if the arbor falls on someone, causing them bodily injury, your insurance would cover their medical expenses. Contact a business insurance agent to discuss what type of insurance policy will be best for your business.

GET A WORK SPACE. When it comes to finding a work space, there are several different options; the most affordable being the home office. Working out of your home allows you to avoid the hefty overhead cost of leasing an office space. In addition, your home office may qualify you for some substantial tax deductions. Having a home office, however, doesn't work for everyone. Another option is to rent or lease a commercial office space. While it may be super empowering to have your own brick and mortar office, this can be quite expensive, and thus difficult to manage when you are just getting your business off the ground. A third option is to rent a shared office space (or coworking space). This is essentially a communal office space shared by other entrepreneurs in various fields. It's more affordable than leasing an entire office, and may be a better option for some than working from home.

KEEP GOOD RECORDS. As a new small business owner, you are already juggling so many different tasks; it can be easy to let your record-keeping slip through the cracks. Try your best not to let this happen! Come up with a schedule for yourself. Pick a day and time that you will dedicate to managing your books every week. This includes all expenses, payments received, mileage, and wages paid (if you have employees). When it comes time to do your taxes (or hand over your books to your CPA), you'll be glad you kept up on it!

DEFINE YOUR SERVICE

Now that you have taken care of all the legal formalities, it's time to work out the details of your service. You'll need to create a clear-cut plan for working with clients, decide what is included in your service (and what is not), and determine what fee you will charge for your service. Remember, you can always make changes to your policies at any time if you feel that a certain policy is not working well for you or your clients. The following questions will help you come up with a clear definition and framework for your service:

- How will you respond to inquiries?

- How and where will the consultation take place? Will it be over the phone or in person? If in person, how far will you travel? Will you charge anything for the consultation or will it be free?

- Once hired, when does your communication with clients officially begin? Will it be limited or unlimited? What methods of communication will you use (email, phone calls, video calls, text messaging, etc.)? Will certain types of communication need to be scheduled in advance (e.g. phone or video calls)?

- Will you have set business hours?

- How many times will you meet with your clients? When will those meetings occur? How far in advance will you schedule your meetings? Where will your meetings take place? Will you put a time cap on your meetings? Will you have a policy on cancellations or no-shows? Will you have a policy on who can attend the meetings?

- When and how will you send your clients the questionnaire? By when will you require your clients have it completed?

- How many hours will you work on the wedding day? Will you offer extended hours for an added fee?

- Will you work by yourself or will you have an assistant?

- Will you help with setup? If so, what items will you help with (e.g. table numbers, menus, wedding favors, escort cards, place cards, signs, guestbook, etc.)?

- Will you help with cleanup? If so, what items will you help with?

- What services are not included (e.g. setting out tables and chairs, cutting the cake, placing linens, taking out garbage, storing or transporting clients' items, etc.)?

- Will you offer any add-on services (e.g. RSVP management, rehearsal dinner coordination, assembling guest welcome bags, etc.)?
- Will you have any involvement after the wedding day (e.g. helping to handle any vendor problems or disputes)?

Other things to consider:

- What will your travel radius be? Will you charge for mileage after a set distance? Will you require overnight accommodations after a set distance? If so, will you book this yourself and bill your clients, or have the clients book this for you?
- What will your backup plan be if you are unable to attend the wedding due to illness, injury, or other unfortunate circumstance?

DETERMINE YOUR FEE. Determining what to charge for your service can be a little unnerving. On the one hand, you don't want to sell yourself short and charge less than what you're worth. On the other hand, without a ton of experience, you don't want to overcharge or you will never attract clients! First, you'll need to determine what the going rate is for wedding coordination in your area. Most coordinators (or planners offering coordination services) will charge between $1000 and $1500, depending on the location and scope of the service. However, it's common (and often necessary) to offer a much lower fee in the early stages of your business to give you an edge over the "competition." If your fee matches those of others in your area, and a prospective client has a choice between the new coordinator with little experience and no reviews, or the experienced coordinator with fifty positive reviews, it's pretty clear who they are going to choose. Lowering your fee will level out the playing field and give potential clients more incentive to give you a shot! As you gain experience, your value to clients will increase, and so, too, should your fee! I'm going to let you in on a little secret. I did my first wedding for $400! Four. Hundred. Dollars! I had no experience and no reviews, so in the eyes of potential clients, I was a risk! I had nothing to back up my claim that I could successfully manage their wedding day. I tried to start my fee at $1000 because *I* knew what I was capable of, but no one would bite, so I began dropping my fee until it became too good for a potential client to pass up! Before long, I booked my very first legit client! Then a few days later, I booked my second client! All it took was finding the right fee. If you have little to no experience, you have to start small. Once those five-star reviews start rolling in, you will be able to increase your fee little by little until you reach your full earning potential!

Here are some additional things you'll want to think about when determining your fee:

- What forms of payment will you accept?
- How much will you require upfront for the deposit?
- What will the client's payment schedule look like and when will the final payment be due?
- Will you charge a late fee for payments made past the due date?
- Will you have a policy in the case of nonpayment?
- Will you charge a flat fee or base your fee on certain factors (e.g. guest count, number of vendors, anticipated amount of work, etc.)?

PREPARE YOUR DOCUMENTS

The last thing you'll need to do before getting started with clients is to prepare all of your documents, handouts, and tools. Here is a list of documents you will need to create for your business (for detailed information on content for these documents, see Chapter 2):

- Consultation Outline Template
- Contract
- Office Policies
- Handouts or Checklists (for your welcome packets)
- Vendor Contact Sheet Template
- Questionnaire
- Rehearsal Outline Template

PRO TIP: Be sure to add your logo to every form or document you create! Not only does it look more professional, but it also gives your brand a stronger presence!

While it may not be the most exciting part about starting your career as a wedding coordinator, accomplishing these steps is a crucial part in starting any formal business. Without them, you risk looking unprofessional at best, and opening yourself up to some serious legal ramifications at worst! By addressing these tasks early on, you can rest easy knowing your foundation is strong and your business is legit! Now let's get you some clients!

FOUR

Getting Clients

WITH A SOLID UNDERSTANDING of the job, and all of the legal formalities addressed, you are now ready to focus on getting clients! In this Chapter, you will learn about how to connect with potential clients, steps you can take to improve your marketability, and ways to attract your very first client!

GET YOUR NAME OUT THERE

You can have all of the talent and expertise in the world, but if potential clients don't know you exist, none of that is going to matter. You'll need to take some steps to ensure that couples who are looking for a wedding coordinator can find you!

CREATE YOUR BUSINESS LISTINGS. The first thing you'll want to do is to get your business listed on online directories, such as Google My Business, Bing, and Yelp. You'll need to create an account with each directory you want to add your business to. Typically, the process involves some sort of verification method (like mailing a verification code to your business address) to ensure you are the true owner of the business. By listing your business on these directories, local couples will be able to find you when they run an online search for wedding coordinators.

CREATE YOUR WEDDING MARKETPLACE PROFILES. A great way to get your name out to potential clients is by creating profiles on online wedding marketplaces, such as The Knot or Wedding Wire. When you are just getting started, these sites can be a great resource for connecting you with potential clients! Most sites will allow you to create a free basic profile page with limited content, with the option of upgrading to a higher membership with added benefits. These benefits typically include more in-depth content, such as pictures and videos, as well as featured placement on search results. However, there is an additional fee you would need to pay in order to access those benefits, so you'll need to weigh your options to figure out which package will be best for your business.

NETWORK. It's never too early to begin building your network! Reach out to some local caterers, florists, photographers, and other wedding vendors to see if they'd be willing to meet you for coffee! Clients will often ask their vendors for referrals when thinking about hiring a wedding coordinator, so by networking with other local vendors, you are creating another avenue to connect with potential clients. The great thing about networking is that it is a two-way street! You are just as likely to lead clients to them as they are to lead clients to you!

Don't be afraid to reach out to other coordinators and planners as well! There is a sentiment embraced by most wedding professionals of "community over competition," meaning that instead of viewing others as competitors, we view each other as sources of encouragement, support, advice, and even assistance at times! Wedding professionals love to help people, it's in our nature! When we can't take on a new client (usually because we're already booked for that date) we love to be able to send that client to another trusted professional. Not only does this help the client, but it also helps out our fellow colleagues (and that includes you)!

BECOME A BRIDAL SHOW VENDOR. Participating in a bridal expo will get you face to face with potentially hundreds of couples who are planning a wedding! In addition, you will be alongside a plethora of experienced wedding vendors with whom you can network! Participating in a bridal show, however, can be costly, with booth fees reaching upwards of several hundred dollars! On top of that, you'll need the supplies to decorate your booth, as well as the marketing material to hand out to prospective clients. Those costs can really add up, so you'll need to think about whether or not the potential gain in business will be worth the investment.

 PRO TIP: Consider creating discount coupons to hand out to interested couples at the bridal show! This is a great way to reel in some of your first clients!

START A BLOG. A great way to get potential clients to your website is by starting a blog! This will help drive traffic to your website by not only putting you higher in search results, but also increasing the number of search terms that will apply to you! For example, let's say you write an article about what wedding coordinators do and post it to your blog. A bride-to-be who is considering hiring a wedding coordinator and wants to learn more about that service runs an online search for "What do wedding coordinators do?" She sees your article in the search results, clicks on it, and now she's on your website! Without your blog, that search would not likely have led to you!

When creating your blog content, consider questions or topics that would be relevant to couples who are thinking of hiring a wedding coordinator! Articles addressing things like "What is wedding coordination?", "What is the difference between a wedding coordinator and a wedding planner?", and "Why you need a wedding coordinator for your wedding?" would be great to include in your blog! You can also include topics that aren't necessarily specific to wedding coordination, but would be something relevant to any couple who is planning a wedding, such as "unique ceremony ideas" or "how to write meaningful wedding vows." The more traffic you drive to your website, the greater chance you have of getting a client out of it!

IMPROVE YOUR MARKETABILITY

In order to make yourself more attractive to potential clients, you will need to improve your marketability. What is marketability? In a nutshell, marketability refers to how likely you are to be hired. How much does your service (and your company in general) appeal to customers? For example, a coordinator with a great amount of experience, a long list of five-star reviews, and a strong social media following is considered highly marketable! On the other hand, a coordinator who has minimal experience, a couple of courtesy reviews from family members, and a limited social media presence has very little marketability. Understanding your marketability will help you determine the steps you need to take to improve your business' appeal to potential clients. While many factors can impact your marketability, the three main areas you'll want to focus on are influence, education, and experience.

INFLUENCE. Social media has become such an important part of running a successful business. Potential clients can learn a lot more about your business from your social media posts than they can from your website, and on a much more personal level! They want to see that you engage with the community; that shows that you are more client-focused. They want to see what kind of content you post; that shows them what's important to you. Social media is about accessability. The more accessible you are, the more transparent you appear, and the more trustworthy you will become in the eyes of prospective clients.

Having a strong social media presence does not happen overnight and involves a lot more than just posting pretty pictures! Your content should be intentional, meaningful, and authentic. Mastering the art of using social media to grow your business takes time and effort. To help you get the most out of your social media marketing, I highly recommend signing up for an online course on creating social media content for wedding professionals.

EDUCATION. To put it simply, potential clients want to know that you know what you're talking about when it comes to weddings. What makes you an expert on the subject? What knowledge or education do you have that will help them? While prospective clients won't typically ask you outright for your educational credentials, they *will* be able to determine your expertise during their interactions with you. Are you using the correct terminology? Are you familiar with the traditional order of events? Are you demonstrating an understanding of their plans and their needs? Without a solid foundation of wedding knowledge, you will have a hard time convincing someone to hire you!

While possessing a degree in hospitality is helpful, there are plenty of other ways to acquire the knowledge needed to be a successful wedding coordinator. One option is to take an online wedding planning course! As a coordinator, understanding the planning process is crucial to helping ensure your clients have a well-thought-out wedding plan. In addition, I would recommend reading books on general wedding etiquette and traditions. Two of my favorites are *The Wedding Book* by Mindy Weiss and *Wedding Etiquette* by Anna Post and Lizzie Post. Having a well-rounded understanding of all things wedding will not only increase your worth to clients, but will ultimately make you more effective as a wedding coordinator.

EXPERIENCE. The most important determinant of your marketability is undoubtedly your level of experience. Everybody knows that while "book knowledge" is essential, the *real* learning happens on the job! Do you have any experience working in the wedding industry? Perhaps you have worked in the catering business or with a florist. This pushes you up a wrung on the marketability ladder. If you're like most people who are just starting out and have little to no experience, you'll want to take some steps to get some practical experience under your belt. Do you have a friend or family member getting married? Maybe even a friend of a friend? If so, offering your services free of charge is a great way to get some real, hands-on experience!

Another way to get some relevant wedding industry experience is to do some work with a caterer. Having this experience myself, I cannot stress enough how useful it was in the beginning stages of my career as a wedding coordinator! The continuous prioritizing and reprioritizing, the thinking on your feet and making decisions under pressure, the hustling and hard work, the teamwork, the dealing with difficult customers, the conflict resolution! All of these skills are so important as a wedding coordinator and without direct experience putting them into practice, you are likely going to feel overwhelmed by the demands of working a wedding, and everything that comes with that role.

Another option for gaining some hands-on experience is to offer assistance to your colleagues. Reach out to the other coordinators and planners in your area and offer to help with the setup of their upcoming weddings! If you do this enough times, you might even be invited to assist for a whole day! What better way to learn the job than by working alongside a seasoned professional?

By implementing these tactics, you will not only better prepare yourself to successfully manage your clients' weddings, you will also increase your value to prospective clients! I highly recommend utilizing one or more of these methods to get yourself some truly practical experience before taking on a paid job. As an added bonus, I have included some tips and bits of advice that only an experienced wedding coordinator would know (see Appendix I)!

LANDING YOUR FIRST CLIENT

You are now ready to take on your very first client! You have your marketplace profiles up and running, your social media pages are gaining traction, and you have a little bit of experience under your belt. You've prepared a solid inquiry response and your fee is set to entice! You might have a few inquiries that go nowhere (this is to be expected, especially in the beginning), but before long you will have a client ready to book a consultation with you! This is where you will have the opportunity to share some real-life experiences and demonstrate your wedding knowledge. In other words, impress them! Draw from your experiences to share some examples of ways you can help them prevent common wedding day mishaps. Be honest about your experience. With a budget-friendly fee and an abundance of practical knowledge to share, it won't be long before a couple recognizes your worth and gives you a chance. And when you *do* get that chance, go the extra mile! Put in some extra hours, offer an additional complimentary meeting with your clients, visit the venue twice if needed! Do whatever it takes to get as much out of this experience as you can by putting as much into it as you can, and in the process, give your clients a positively unforgettable wedding day!

Conclusion

You now have all the information you need to start your career as a wedding coordinator! You've learned all about what a wedding coordinator is, what a wedding coordinator does, what a wedding coordinator shouldn't do, and the basic steps for managing a wedding from beginning to end. You've also learned various things to consider when working with clients to ensure they have given adequate thought to every detail of their day. We discussed ways to formalize your business and steps you can take to attract more clients. With all of this information at your fingertips, starting your wedding coordinating business should be a piece of three-tiered salted caramel and vanilla buttercream filled wedding cake!

Appendices

APPENDIX A

SAMPLE INQUIRY RESPONSE

"Hello Elizabeth!

Thank you so much for reaching out to me and congratulations on your engagement!!

Here is the information you requested. My coordination package includes one planning meeting (up to 3 hours long), unlimited communication via phone or email (starting 2 months out from your wedding), facilitation of the rehearsal, and up to 12 hours of service on your wedding day! I'll begin by collecting any and all contracts you currently have with your vendors. This helps me gain a better understanding of your plans for your big day! At 2 months out, I will send you a questionnaire to fill out. It's very thorough and really helps to identify any areas or details that may have been overlooked or need further attention. We will schedule our planning meeting for roughly 3 to 5 weeks out from the wedding date. During our meeting, we will comb through EVERYTHING! :) We will talk through every little detail to help ensure your day is meticulously planned!

After our meeting, I will reach out to each vendor to ensure everyone is on the same page and to answer any questions they may have. With all of this information, I will put together a very detailed timeline that lays out every step of your day! Once it's complete, I'll send it to you for approval, and once approved, I will send it off to all relevant vendors. I will help run the rehearsal (often in tandem with the officiant) to ensure everyone knows their placement and roles, and is comfortable with how the ceremony will run. On the wedding day, I will be there to make sure all of your plans play out the way they are supposed to! :) The timeline helps me to stay 2 steps ahead of everyone else so that I can be sure that everyone is ready and on cue for each step of the day!

This package starts at $xxxx. While I do most weddings by myself, I do have an assistant that I bring on in certain cases. Things like a large amount of décor to set up, a large guest list, or a short setup time frame could require that I bring my assistant on board. This would increase the cost by $xxx.

I'd love to hear more about your plans and to answer any questions you have! If you are interested in setting up a time to chat just let me know your availability and we can get that scheduled!

Thank you again for reaching out! I look forward to hearing back from you!"

APPENDIX B

SAMPLE CONSULTATION QUESTIONNAIRE

Names:

      Client A: _____

      Client B: _____

Wedding Date: _____

Ceremony Location: _____

Ceremony Time: _____

Cocktail Hour Location: _____

Cocktail Hour Time: _____

Reception Location: _____

Reception Time: _____

Rehearsal Date: _____

Estimated Guest Count: _____

Vendors booked:

-    _____
-    _____
-    _____
-    _____
-    _____

Vendors needed:

-    _____
-    _____
-    _____

- _____
- _____

How many people are in your wedding party? _____

What are the general décor plans (as well as the desired style, look, and atmosphere)?

_____
_____
_____

What time does the venue open for access? _____

What time does the venue close? _____

What is your biggest worry or concern about your wedding day?

_____

Notes:

_____
_____
_____
_____

APPENDIX C

TIME-SAVING SETUP TIPS
(TO HAVE YOUR CLIENTS DO)

- Remove all décor from its original packaging
- Preplace batteries in all battery-operated items
- Put escort cards in alphabetical order (by last name)
- Put place cards in groupings organized by table
- Pre-fold any paper goods that require folding (e.g. tented escort cards or menus)
- Preplace candles in holders, if possible
- Position any candle wicks so they are pointed straight up
- Pre-fold napkins, if providing own
- Pack décor in boxes organized by placement (e.g. guestbook table décor, ceremony décor, centerpiece items, etc.)
- Label décor boxes
- Include detailed instructions for placement of décor
- If part of the setup includes filling anything with water, pack a water pitcher

APPENDIX D

SAMPLE VENDOR CONTACT SHEET

Vendor Contact Sheet

Vendor	Company	Contact	Number	Email	Contract
Venue	Rosewood Event Center	Stephanie Moore	(555) 555-5555	email@email.com	☐
Caterer	Rosewood Catering	Justin Lang	(555) 555-4444	email@email.com	☐
Bartenders					☐
Cake/Desserts					☐
Florist					☐
Photographer					☐
Band/DJ					☐
Rentals					☐
Videographer					☐
Transportation					☐
Hair/Makeup					☐
Officiant					☐
Other:					☐
Other:					☐
Other:					☐

APPENDIX E

SAMPLE WEDDING DAY QUESTIONNAIRE

ELIZABETH & SCOTT
AUGUST 3, 2019

Estimated guest count: _____

Rehearsal date/time/location: _____

Do you have a date set for getting your marriage license?

       Yes   No

       If yes, please list date: _____

Have you purchased event liability insurance?

       Yes   No

PRE-CEREMONY

Where will you be staying the night before the wedding?

       Bride: _____

       Groom: _____

What are your morning plans on the day of your wedding (e.g. meeting for breakfast/coffee, together/separate, etc.)?

       Bride: _____

       Groom: _____

Will the bride be getting her hair done by a stylist?	Yes	No
Bridesmaids?	Yes	No
Others?	Yes	No

Total number getting hair done: _____

Names: _____

Location: _____

Start Time: _____ End Time: _____

Will the bride be getting makeup done by a makeup artist?   Yes   No

Bridesmaids?   Yes   No

Others?   Yes   No

Total number getting makeup done: _____

Names: _____

Location: _____

Start Time: _____ End Time: _____

What are your lunch plans for the wedding day (e.g. having lunch delivered, bringing sandwiches to salon, etc.)?

      Bride: _____

      Groom: _____

Where will you be getting dressed? Please include time(s), if known.

      Bride: _____ Groom: _____

      Bridesmaids: _____ Groomsmen: _____

How will you be getting to the ceremony site (e.g. driving self, riding with someone, limo, etc.)? Please list departure time(s), if known.

      Bride: _____ Groom: _____

      Bridesmaids: _____ Groomsmen: _____

What time do you plan to arrive at the ceremony site?

      Bride: _____ Groom: _____

      Bridesmaids: _____ Groomsmen: _____

Are you planning on having your photographer capture "getting ready" photos?

      Yes   No

Will you be doing a "first look" with your photographer?

      Yes   No

      If yes, please list location: _____

Do you plan on having any formal portraits done *before* the ceremony (bride w/ bridesmaids, groom w/ groomsmen, etc.)?

      Yes   No

      If yes, please list:

_____ _____

_____ _____

_____ _____

CEREMONY

Ceremony Location: _____

Ceremony Start Time: _____

WEDDING PARTY
- Maid/Matron of Honor: _____
- Bridesmaids:
  - _____
  - _____
  - _____
  - _____
  - _____
  - _____
- Best Man: _____
- Groomsmen:
  - _____
  - _____
  - _____
  - _____
  - _____
  - _____
- Flower Girl(s): _____
- Ring Bearer(s): _____
- Ushers:
  - _____

     ○   _____

- Any other participants in the wedding ceremony (not including offici-ant; e.g. readers, singers, etc.)?
  Name/Role:
    - _____
    - _____
- Officiant: _____

Please indicate the order in which you would like your wedding party to stand at the altar by writing in their first names or initials in the spaces below (O=Officiant, B=Bride, G=Groom):

O

___ ___ ___ ___ ___ ___ B   G ___ ___ ___ ___ ___ ___

ORDER OF EVENTS

Below is the standard order of events for a wedding ceremony, for reference. However, this is YOUR day and every bit of it should represent who you are as a couple. So, in the space to the right, please share an outline of your unique, creative, special, or otherwise awesome ceremony plans! And don't worry, even if it follows the "standard" order, it will still be special, personal, and AMAZING!

STANDARD CEREMONY
- Processional
- Officiant's Opening Words
- Statement of Intention
- Charge to the Couple
- Exchange of Vows
- Ring Exchange
- Officiant's Closing Remarks
- Pronouncement of Marriage
- Kiss
- Presentation of the Couple
- Recessional

YOUR AWESOME CEREMONY
-
-
-
-
-
-
-
-
-
-
-

PROCESSIONAL

Here are two versions of a standard processional:

• Seating of the Special Guests	• Seating of the Special Guests
• Officiant and Groom enter from side	• Officiant, Groom, and Groomsmen enter from side
• Bridesmaids/Groomsmen	• Bridesmaids
• Maid of Honor/Best Man	• Maid of Honor
• Ring Bearer	• Ring Bearer
• Flower Girl	• Flower Girl
• Bride and Escort	• Bride and Escort

There are limitless options for the processional, so please answer the following questions:

Would the groom prefer to enter from the side at the beginning of the ceremony, or walk down the aisle as part of the processional (he could walk alone or be escorted by one or both of his parents during the seating of the special guests)?

Please list preference: _____

Would you prefer the groomsmen to be standing at the altar (entering from the side), walking solo down the aisle, or escorting the bridesmaids down the aisle during the processional?

Please list preference: _____

Would you like the officiant to enter from the side or walk down the aisle as part of the processional?

Please list preference: _____

SEATING OF THE SPECIAL GUESTS

Would you like any special guests formally seated before the wedding party walks down the aisle (could be parents of the groom, mother of the bride, grandparents, etc.; escorts could be relatives, friends, or ushers)?

Please list special guests to be formally seated:

• _____ escorted by _____

- _____ escorted by _____
- _____ escorted by _____
- _____ escorted by _____

Who is escorting the bride down the aisle? _____

PROCESSIONAL SONGS

Please list your song choices for the processional, along with whom the song should accompany (typically the special guests are seated while the prelude music is still playing, so you do not *have* to specify a song for the special guests, unless of course you want to! More commonly, you will have one song for the wedding party, and one special song for the bride).

Song: _____ For Whom: _____

Song: _____ For Whom: _____

Song: _____ For Whom: _____

RECESSIONAL

The standard recessional is as follows:

- Bride and Groom
- Flower Girl/Ring Bearer (optional)
- Maid of Honor/Best Man
- Bridesmaids/Groomsmen
- Brides Parents (optional)
- Grooms Parents (optional)

Would you like to formally include your parents in the recessional (the officiant will typically walk up and excuse the bride's parents first, and the groom's parents second)?

Bride: Yes   No   Names: _____

Groom: Yes   No   Names: _____

Recessional Song: _____

ADDITIONAL CEREMONY QUESTIONS

Will your ceremony have a religious affiliation?

Yes   No

If yes, please list religion: _____

Will you be incorporating a unity ceremony of any kind (unity candle, wine ceremony, tree planting ceremony, sand ceremony, etc.)?

Yes   No

If yes, please list: _____

If utilizing a ring bearer in your ceremony, will he be carrying the actual rings?

Yes   No

If yes, who will he bring the rings to (best man, officiant, etc.)?

_____

If no, who will be holding the rings during the ceremony?

_____

What will the ring bearer be carrying (box, pillow, etc.)?

_____

If utilizing a flower girl, will she be dropping flower petals?

Yes   No

What will the flower girl be carrying (basket, bouquet, etc.)?

_____

Will you have wedding programs?

Yes   No

If yes, who is responsible for handing them out? _____

Will there be a microphone/sound system for the ceremony?

Yes   No

If yes, what type of microphone will be used for the ceremony (lapel, wireless, stand or no stand)? _____

Would you like your officiant to make any announcements after the ceremony? It may be helpful to have your officiant give the guests some information on

what is happening next, or where they should go after the ceremony.
Announcements:

_____

_____

Please list any additional information regarding the ceremony you feel is relevant:

_____

_____

_____

COCKTAIL HOUR

Will you be having a cocktail hour after your ceremony?
Yes   No

Cocktail hour location: _____

Cocktail hour start time: _____

How long would you prefer your cocktail hour to last? I recommend no longer than one and a half hours, as guests tend to get a little bored and hungry (and possibly tipsy) if it lasts much longer than that! Typically, if you are doing a first look and getting portraits done before the ceremony, then I recommend an hour. If there is no first look, or very few portraits are being done before the ceremony, then I recommend an hour and a half.
Preferred length of time for cocktail hour: _____

Will there be a bar open during cocktail hour?
Yes   No

Will there be hors d'oeuvres available during cocktail hour?
Yes   No
If yes, will they be stationed or passed? _____

Will the bride and groom (or anyone else) be going anywhere off-site for photos during cocktail hour?

      Yes   No

      If yes, please list where and when: _____

Please list any additional information regarding the cocktail hour you feel is relevant:

_____

_____

_____

RECEPTION

Reception location: _____

Reception start time: _____

Below is the standard order of events for a wedding reception, for reference. In the space to the right, please list your preference for the order of events for *your* reception.

STANDARD RECEPTION	YOUR AWESOME RECEPTION
• Grand Entrance/Introductions	•
• Grace/Blessing	•
• Dinner Served/Buffet	•
• Toasts	•
• First Dance	•
• Father/Daughter Dance	•
• Mother/Son Dance	•
• Cake Cutting/Dessert	•
• Open Dancing	•
• Bouquet/Garter Toss	•
• Open Dancing	•
• Last Dance	•
• Grand Exit	•

RECEIVING LINE
Are you interested in having a receiving line at any point during your wedding day?

Yes   No

GRAND ENTRANCE/INTRODUCTIONS
Are you planning on having a grand entrance with introductions?

Yes   No

STANDARD ORDER FOR INTRODUCTIONS:	WHO YOU WOULD LIKE INTRODUCED:
• Bride's Parents (optional)	•
• Groom's Parents (optional)	•
• Flower Girl/Ring Bearer (opt.)	•
• Bridesmaids/Groomsmen	•
• Maid of Honor/Best Man	•
• Bride and Groom	•

Please indicate how you would like each person/pair formally introduced, including you (e.g. first names only, first and last, any special titles, Mr. and Mrs., etc.):

• _____

• _____

• _____

• _____

• _____

• _____

• _____

• _____

Who will be making the introductions? _____

Do you have any special song selections for the introductions? Typically, there is one for the wedding party (with or without parents) and one for the bride and groom. Some choose to pick a unique song for each person or pair being introduced.

Song: _____ For Whom: _____
Song: _____ For Whom: _____
Song: _____ For Whom: _____

SONG SELECTIONS
Please list your choice of song (with artist) for each event listed below that will
be a part of your wedding reception. For certain events (i.e. cake cutting,
bouquet/garter toss, anniversary dance, etc.) it is not required that you choose a
specific song. You may wish to leave the song choice up to the musician or DJ.

- Bride/Groom First Dance   Song: _____
- Father/Daughter Dance   Song: _____
- Mother/Son Dance   Song: _____
- Other: _____ /_____ Dance   Song: _____
- Cake Cutting   Song: _____
- Bouquet Toss   Song: _____
- Garter Toss   Song: _____
- Anniversary Dance   Song: _____
- Last Song   Song: _____
- Other: _____   Song: _____

ADDITIONAL RECEPTION QUESTIONS

Will someone be offering a prayer or blessing before dinner service?
    Yes   No
    If yes, who: _____

What type of dinner service will you be having (plated, family style, buffet, etc.)?
_____

Will there be assigned seating?
    Yes   No
    If yes, will the guests be assigned to a table or to a specific chair?
_____

Do you have a floor plan?

       Yes   No

Do you have a seating chart?

       Yes   No

Will you have escort cards or a seating assignment board*? _____

*Escort cards are typically on a table by the entrance of the reception space and include each guest's name and assigned table number. Some choose to use a seating assignment board instead of escort cards, which lists each guest's name in alphabetical order followed by the table number they are assigned to. Place cards (also called name cards) are set on the guest tables informing the guests of which specific *seat* they are assigned to.

How will they be displayed? _____

Who will cut the cake for the guests? _____

Do you have a cake knife and server?

       Yes   No

Will you be saving any cake (e.g. to freeze for anniversary)?

       Yes   No

Have you included your vendors in your meal count?

       Yes   No

       Total number of vendors needing a meal: _____

Is there a designated place for vendors to sit during dinner?

       Yes   No

       If yes, please indicate where: _____

Will anyone be giving a toast or speech?

       Yes   No

If yes, who? Please list in order you'd like them to speak:

1. _____

2. _____

3. _____

4. _____

Would you (the Bride and/or Groom) like to say anything to your guests after the toasts? This is entirely optional, but it is a great opportunity to thank everyone for coming!

    Yes   No

Will you have a champagne pour?

    Yes   No

    If yes, please list for whom (all guests, wedding party only, bride/groom only, etc.):

    _____

Will you be doing a grand exit?

    Yes   No

    Will guests have bubbles, sparklers, or any other item for the grand exit?

    Please list: _____

Would you like to keep any floral arrangements?

    Yes   No

    If yes, please specify:

    _____

    _____

Are there any other disposable items you wish to keep (e.g. place cards, menus, etc.)?

    Yes   No

    If yes, please specify:

    _____

At the end of the evening, I will help collect your personal décor items (i.e. centerpiece items, signage, small accent décor pieces, etc.), however, you will need to designate at least 2 people who will be responsible for removing the items from the venue. Please identify who will be responsible for taking the following items with them at the end of the night:

Gifts/Cards: _____

Décor: _____

Leftovers: _____

Will there be any rented items that you will need to return?

Yes   No

If yes, please list items: _____

Please list any special packing requirements for these items:

_____

Please list any additional information regarding the reception you feel is relevant:

_____

_____

_____

DÉCOR CHECKLIST

Please check the box next to each item you plan on utilizing in your wedding décor. Feel free to write in any notes you feel would be helpful for me to know (specific location of item, placement, color of item, who is providing, total number of items, etc).

CEREMONY

☐ Seating

    ☐ Chairs

        ☐ Chair sashes

        ☐ Chair florals

    ☐ Benches/pews

- ☐ Altar
    - ☐ Arbor
        - ☐ Arbor floral
        - ☐ Backdrop
        - ☐ Draping
    - ☐ Unity Table
        - ☐ Unity ceremony item(s)
        - ☐ Linen
        - ☐ Other items:
    - ☐ Other altar décor:
- ☐ Aisle
    - ☐ Aisle runner
    - ☐ Candles/lanterns
    - ☐ Floral arrangements/petals
    - ☐ Doors/curtains
    - ☐ Other aisle décor:

COCKTAIL HOUR
- ☐ Tables
    - ☐ Linens
    - ☐ Centerpieces
        - ☐ Floral arrangements
        - ☐ Candles/lanterns
        - ☐ Other table décor:
- ☐ Chairs
- ☐ Lounge furniture
- ☐ Gift table
    - ☐ Linen
    - ☐ Card box
    - ☐ Gift table décor
- ☐ Guestbook table
    - ☐ Linen
    - ☐ Guestbook/pens
    - ☐ Guestbook table décor

☐ Other cocktail hour décor:

RECEPTION
- ☐ Escort cards
- ☐ Head table or sweetheart table
  - ☐ Linens/runners/overlays
  - ☐ Centerpieces
    - ☐ Floral arrangements
    - ☐ Candles/lanterns
    - ☐ Other:
  - ☐ Other head table/sweetheart table décor:
- ☐ Guest tables
  - ☐ Linens/runners/overlays
  - ☐ Centerpieces
    - ☐ Floral arrangements
    - ☐ Candles/lanterns
    - ☐ Other:
  - ☐ Other guest table décor:
- ☐ Table numbers/table number holders
- ☐ Charger plates
- ☐ Linen napkins
  - ☐ Fold style: _____
- ☐ Menus
- ☐ Place cards
- ☐ Chairs
  - ☐ Chair sashes
  - ☐ Chair florals
- ☐ Entrance décor
- ☐ Cake/dessert table
  - ☐ Linen
  - ☐ Cake/dessert stands or trays
  - ☐ Other dessert table décor:
- ☐ Wedding favor table
  - ☐ Linen

- ☐ Wedding favors
  - ☐ Other wedding favor table décor:
- ☐ Uplighting
- ☐ Photo backdrop
  - ☐ Photo props
- ☐ Other reception décor:

SIGNAGE

- ☐ Welcome sign
- ☐ Program sign
- ☐ Parking sign
- ☐ Ceremony "this way" sign
- ☐ "Gifts/Cards" sign (for gift table)
- ☐ "Sign Our Guestbook" sign
- ☐ Hashtag sign
- ☐ Seating assignment board
- ☐ Bar menu
- ☐ Dessert table sign
- ☐ Wedding favors sign
- ☐ Other signage:
- ☐ Easels/stands for signs

APPENDIX F

SAMPLE TIMELINE

THE WEDDING OF

Elizabeth DeYoung & Scott Gordon

AUGUST 3, 2019
ROSEWOOD EVENT CENTER

7:50 a.m.   Elizabeth, Meredith, Lena, Kenzie, Aria, Kristen, and Kimberly meet at Rosewood Salon for hair/makeup

	Makeup		Hair
8:00 AM	Kenzie	8:00 AM	Elizabeth (curl)
8:30 AM	Lena	8:40 AM	Aria
9:00 AM	Meredith	9:20 AM	Kristen
9:45 AM	Elizabeth	10:00 AM	Kenzie
10:30 AM	Aria	10:40 AM	Lena
11:00 AM	Kristen	11:20 AM	Elizabeth
11:30 AM	Kimberly	12:20 PM	Kimberly
12:30 PM	Elizabeth (touch up)	1:00 PM	Meredith

9:00 a.m.   Venue opens for access
- Tables and chairs set
- Linens pressed and placed on tables
- Napkins folded and set on tables

Mark delivers décor and sets up lights on patio

Rental company delivers and sets up arbor

11:00 a.m.   Florist arrives and begins setup of reception space

- Centerpieces on guest tables
- Small arrangement for gift table
- Small arrangement for guestbook table
- Loose greenery (for baker to add to cake)

12:00 p.m.   Allison arrives at REC and begins setup of decor
- Ceremony
  - Shepherd's hooks with lanterns down aisle
  - Unity candles/lighter on table at altar
  - Reserved signs for front 2 rows
  - Welcome sign/easel
- Cocktail Hour
  - Small lanterns on cocktail tables
  - LED candles on stairs
  - Guestbook/marker/sign on table
- Reception
  - Table numbers
  - Menus
  - Escort cards
  - Place cards
  - Votives on guest tables
  - LED candles on bar
  - "Gifts/Cards" sign on gift table + LED candles
  - Wedding favors on guest tables

Scott and groomsmen meet at Rosewood Bar and Grill for lunch

Meredith picks up lunch from Rosewood Café and brings back to salon

12:30 p.m.   Florist begins setup of ceremony and cocktail hour spaces
- Garland on arbor

- Loose greenery in aisle lanterns
- Greenery above welcome sign
- Loose greenery in cocktail table lanterns

1:40 p.m.	Ladies are finished with hair/makeup and travel to rental cottage to get dressed
	Scott and groomsmen meet at Rosewood Inn to begin getting ready
2:00 p.m.	Ladies arrive at rental cottage, bridesmaids get dressed
	Caterers arrive at REC and begin setting tables
2:30 p.m.	Photographer (Jenna) arrives at ladies' cottage, Assistant (Kris) arrives at guys' hotel room; photographers capture getting ready shots
	Florist delivers bouquets and corsages to ladies at cottage
2:45 p.m.	Elizabeth puts on dress; photos with Mom
2:50 p.m.	Florist delivers boutonnieres to guys at hotel
	Photographer (Kris) gets portraits of groom and groomsmen
3:00 p.m.	Photographer (Jenna) gets portraits of bride and bridesmaids
	DJ (Brad) arrives at REC and begins setup
	Baker delivers and sets up cake; adds greenery
3:20 p.m.	Shuttle 1 arrives at Rosewood Inn to pick up guys

	Jerry drives to REC, brings remaining boutonnieres
3:30 p.m.	Scott and groomsmen arrive at REC, wait in Conference Room 3
	Shuttle 2 arrives at rental cottage to pick up ladies
	Kimberly drives to REC, brings remaining corsage
	Bartenders arrive and begin setup
3:50 p.m.	Elizabeth and bridesmaids arrive at REC, wait in Bridal Suite
4:00 p.m.	Shuttles 1 and 2 arrive at Rosewood Inn to pick up guests
4:20 p.m.	Shuttles 1 and 2 depart Rosewood Inn, travel to REC
4:25 p.m.	Ushers (Anthony, Jacob, and Lance) take places near REC entrance
4:30 p.m.	Pastor John arrives at REC
	Allison pins boutonnieres on Pastor John, Father of the Bride (Mark), and Ring Bearers (Gabe and Henry)
	Allison gives corsage to Mother of the Groom (Heather)

Final preparations:
- Make sure all ceremony items are in place
- Make sure Pastor John gets lapel mic
- Make sure handheld mic is on ceremony table
- Make sure Ring Bearer has ring box/rings
- Make sure Flower Girls have baskets/petals
- Make sure wagon is at base of wooden steps

	Prelude music begins
	Guests arrive at REC
4:35 p.m.	Ushers collect gifts and cards and escort guests to the ceremony location
4:50 p.m.	Allison lines up Attendants

- At base of wooden steps:
  - Grandparents of Groom: Marvin & Rena/Brent
  - Grandmother of Bride: Doris/Mitch
  - Grandparents of Bride: George & Nancy/Grant
  - Parents of Groom: Jerry & Heather/Scott
  - Mother of Bride: Kimberly/Jamari
  - Pastor John (Scott will join after seating Jerry & Heather)
- At top of wooden stairs:
  - Kristen & Brandon
  - Aria & Parker
  - Kenzie & Niall
  - Lena & Taylor
  - Sam (Mitch will join after seating Doris)
  - Meredith (Jamari will join after seating Kimberly)
  - Ring Bearers: Gabe and Henry
  - Flower Girls: Eleanor, Gigi, and Grace
- Inside venue:
  - Elizabeth and Mark (Father)

5:00 p.m.	Seating of the Special Guests

- Marvin & Rena, escorted by Brent

- Doris, escorted by Mitch
  - Mitch returns to line to join Sam
- George & Nancy, escorted by Grant
- Jerry & Heather, escorted by Scott
  - Scott returns to line to join Pastor John
- Kimberly, escorted by Jamari
  - Jamari returns to line to join Meredith

Groom and Officiant
- Pastor John and Scott walk down aisle and take places at altar

Wedding Party
*Song – *Just the Way You Are* by The Piano Guys
- Kristen & Brandon
- Aria & Parker
- Kenzie & Niall
- Lena & Taylor
- Sam & Mitch
- Meredith & Jamari
- Ring Bearers: Gabe and Henry
- Flower Girls: Eleanor, Gigi, and Grace

Pastor John asks guests to please rise

Bride
*Song – *A Thousand Years* by Christina Perri
- Elizabeth walks down aisle escorted by her father, Mark

Pastor John leads ceremony
- Opening Remarks
- Prayer
- Scripture

- Charge to the Couple
- Declaration of Consent
- Vows
- Rings
- Scripture
- Unity Candle
- Reading: Aunt Becca
- Prayer
- Pronouncement of Marriage
- Kiss
- Presentation of the Couple: "Mr. & Mrs. Scott and Elizabeth Gordon"

5:30 p.m.   Recessional
*Song – *Spring* by Antonio Vivaldi
- Elizabeth & Scott
- Meredith & Jamari
- Sam & Mitch
- Lena & Taylor
- Kenzie & Niall
- Aria & Parker
- Kristen & Brandon

Pastor John dismisses parents
- Bride's Parents: Mark and Kimberly
- Groom's Parents: Jerry and Heather

Ushers dismiss guests

5:35 p.m.   Cocktail hour begins

DJ begins cocktail hour music

Bar opens (outdoor bar on patio and indoor bar)

Hors d'oeuvres passed by catering staff

Group photos at ceremony site
- o Family
- o Wedding Party
- o Bride and Groom

6:00 p.m.   Bride/Groom photos around property

6:30 p.m.   DJ asks guests to begin finding their seats

6:40 p.m.   Bar closes

Allison lines up Parents and Wedding Party for introductions
- Bride's parents: Mark & Kimberly
- Groom's parents: Jerry & Heather
- Kristen & Brandon
- Aria & Parker
- Kenzie & Niall
- Lena & Taylor
- Sam & Mitch
- Meredith & Jamari (with kids)
- Elizabeth & Scott

6:50 p.m.   DJ announces arrival of wedding party and begins
introductions
*Song – *I Gotta Feeling* by Black Eyed Peas

Parents
- Bride's Parents: Mr. & Mrs. Mark and Kimberly DeYoung
- Groom's Parents: Mr. & Mrs. Jerry and Heather Gordon

Bridesmaids/Groomsmen
- Kristen White and Brandon Keil
- Aria and Parker McGinnis
- Kenzie Mathis and Niall Adams
- Lena Munshi and Taylor Ross
- Sam Stiles and Mitch Orbison
- Matron of Honor and Best Man: Meredith and Jamari Sall, accompanied by Ring Bearers: Gabe and Henry, and Flower Girls: Eleanor, Gigi, and Grace

Bride/Groom
- "Mr. and Mrs. Scott and Elizabeth Gordon"

7:00 p.m.	DJ introduces Father of the Groom, Jerry Gordon, for the blessing
	Caterers serve salads
	Bartenders pour champagne
7:20 p.m.	Toasts • Father of the Bride, Mark DeYoung • Matron of Honor, Meredith Sall • Best Man, Jamari Sall Bride & Groom Speech • Elizabeth and Scott
7:40 p.m.	Dinner buffet is open; caterers will release tables
7:50 p.m.	Bar opens after Bride, Groom, and Wedding Party get dinner
8:50 p.m.	First Dance *Song – Make You Feel My Love by Adele

8:55 p.m.	Father/Daughter Dance
	Song – What a Wonderful World by Louis Armstrong
9:00 p.m.	Mother/Son Dance
	Song – You'll Be in My Heart by Phil Collins
9:05 p.m.	Elizabeth and Scott cut cake
	Song – Cake by the Ocean by DNCE
	Caterers slice cake and set on dessert table
	DJ announces guests may help themselves to dessert
9:15 p.m.	Open dancing
9:45 p.m.	Bouquet Toss
	Song – All the Single Ladies by Beyonce
	Garter Toss
	Song – Pour Some Sugar on Me by Def Leppard
10:00 p.m.	Open dancing
10:30 p.m.	Caterers serve pizza snack
	Check in with Jamari on car decorating
11:00 p.m.	Allison begins packing decor
11:15 p.m.	Jamari brings Scott's car up to the main entrance
	DJ asks guests to meet at the main entrance for a sparkler send-off

11:30 p.m.	Sparkler Grand Exit
11:40 p.m.	Elizabeth and Scott depart
	Photographer departs
	Bartenders clear all remaining glassware
	Bride's parents taking centerpieces, décor, and leftover desserts
	Groom's parents taking gifts and cards
12:00 a.m.	Venue closes
	All vendors depart

APPENDIX G

SAMPLE REHEARSAL OUTLINE

THE WEDDING REHEARSAL OF

Elizabeth & Scott

1) INTRODUCTIONS/OVERVIEW

2) LINE UP THE WEDDING PARTY FOR THE CEREMONY

Pastor John

Elizabeth   Scott

KW – AM – KM – LM – SS – MS   JS – MD – TR – NA – PM – BK

3) PRACTICE THE RECESSIONAL
   *Song – *Spring* by Antonio Vivaldi
   - Elizabeth & Scott
   - Meredith & Jamari
   - Sam & Mitch
   - Lena & Taylor
   - Kenzie & Niall
   - Aria & Parker
   - Kristen & Brandon

Pastor John dismisses parents
   - Bride's parents: Mark and Kimberly
   - Groom's parents: Jerry and Heather

4) PRACTICE THE PROCESSIONAL
   - Line up Attendants:
     o At base of wooden steps:

- Grandparents of Groom: Marvin & Rena/Brent
- Grandmother of Bride: Doris/Mitch
- Grandparents of Bride: George & Nancy/Grant
- Parents of Groom: Jerry & Heather/Scott
- Mother of Bride: Kimberly/Jamari
- Pastor John (Scott will join after seating Jerry & Heather)

- At top of wooden stairs:
  - Kristen & Brandon
  - Aria & Parker
  - Kenzie & Niall
  - Lena & Taylor
  - Sam (Mitch will join after seating Doris)
  - Meredith (Jamari will join after seating Kimberly)
  - Ring Bearers: Gabe and Henry
  - Flower Girls: Eleanor, Gigi, and Grace

- Inside venue:
  - Elizabeth and Mark (Father)

- Processional
  - Seating of the Special Guests
    - Marvin & Rena, escorted by Brent
    - Doris, escorted by Mitch
      - Mitch returns to line to join Sam
    - George & Nancy, escorted by Grant
    - Jerry & Heather, escorted by Scott
      - Scott returns to line to join Pastor John
    - Kimberly, escorted by Jamari
      - Jamari returns to line to join Meredith

- o Groom and Officiant
  - Pastor John and Scott walk down aisle and take places at altar

- o Wedding Party
  *Song – *Just the Way You Are* by The Piano Guys
  - Kristen & Brandon
  - Aria & Parker
  - Kenzie & Niall
  - Lena & Taylor
  - Sam & Mitch
  - Meredith & Jamari
  - Ring Bearers: Gabe and Henry
  - Flower Girls: Eleanor, Gigi, and Grace

  Pastor John asks guests to rise

- o Bride and Father
  *Song – *A Thousand Years* by Christina Perri
  - Elizabeth, escorted by Mark

5) REVIEW THE CEREMONY

- Opening Remarks
- Prayer
- Scripture
- Charge to the Couple
- Declaration of Consent
- Vows
- Rings
- Scripture
- Unity Candle
- Reading: Aunt Becca
- Prayer

- Pronouncement of Marriage
- Kiss
- Presentation of the Couple

6) COMPLETE RUN-THROUGH

APPENDIX H

HOW TO COORDINATE A STYLED SHOOT

1.   COME UP WITH A DESIGN PLAN

Start by jotting down some ideas for your design concept. This could mean making a list of terms that describe your desired look, putting together some color swatches, or sketching out a tablescape. Pull together a collection of wedding images that inspire you and focus on narrowing down your color palette. Once you have landed on a color palette, start working on the details of your design. What types of scenes do you want to create? A ceremony scene? A reception scene? Both? What do you envision for each of the scenes you wish to create? What look are you going for? What items will you need in order to accomplish that look? What vendors will you need to bring on board? Once you have a solid direction for your styled shoot, start thinking about where it will happen!

2.   SECURE A VENUE AND A DATE

The next step is to figure out when and where your styled shoot will take place! Research all the venues in your area to find the ones that fit the theme of your styled shoot. Reach out to the venue manager at each location that interests you to see if they'd allow you to hold your styled shoot there in exchange for the photos acquired from the shoot. If you plan on submitting the photos to any blogs, be sure to mention that in your communications! An opportunity to potentially get published is a great selling point to get vendors on board! Once you've nailed down the venue, you'll be able to work with the manager to figure out a date that works for both of you.

3.   FIND A PHOTOGRAPHER

Now that you have a solid plan for your styled shoot, as well as a venue and a date, you'll need to find a photographer. Research the photographers in your area to find ones whose work complements the style of your shoot. Some photographers have a more "light and airy" style while others have a richer, deeper, more "moody" tone to their images. Reach out to the photographers you like and see if they'd be interested in joining you! Photographers have no shortage of images to use for marketing, so in order to gain their interest you'll want to be sure you are creating something unique and original.

4. PULL TOGETHER THE REST OF THE TEAM

With a photographer on board, you'll have an easier time recruiting the other vendors that you need. Start contacting your top picks for a florist, baker, bridal boutique, rental company, hair stylist, etc. You'll also want to start searching for models for your styled shoot! See if any of your friends or family members would be willing to help you out! If not, try posting a model call on your social media pages. Most people would jump at the opportunity for a free photo shoot!

5. MEET WITH VENDORS TO WORK OUT DETAILS

Start setting up meetings with your vendors to discuss more in-depth plans for your styled shoot. You'll want to create a document with each vendors' name and information on it to share with all of the vendors. It is helpful to also include the details of what each vendor is providing. This will help to keep you organized and can also help all of the vendors have a more unified understanding of the design plan. At each of your meetings, be sure to bring your color swatches as well as any inspirational images you've collected (aka your mood board). Together with your vendor team, you will turn your vision into a tangible plan!

6. CREATE A SCHEDULE FOR THE DAY OF THE SHOOT

Put together a timeline for your styled shoot. Include any and all tasks that will need to be accomplished that day (e.g. "pick up suit at 9:00 a.m." or "rentals arriving at 10:30 a.m."). Make sure you include a shot list of all the images you want the photographer to capture, such as an invitation flat lay, shot of the bride's and groom's shoes, or aerial view of the head table. Just like on a wedding day, things will move very quickly on the day of the shoot and you don't want to miss out on getting any of the photos you envisioned! Share your timeline with all of the vendors so they have an idea of how the day will run as well.

7.   PULL IT OFF!

Make sure you have everything packed up and ready to go the day before the shoot. Once you've arrived at the venue, get started right away with any setup you have! Be sure to stick to your schedule so everything rolls out smoothly and nothing gets forgotten. Trust in your photographer and do your best not to give them too much instruction. They know what they're doing and will likely have some pretty amazing ideas of their own to add to your shot list!

After all of the vendors have worked their magic and things have wrapped up, be sure to thank everyone for their contributions. Just like you, many of them will be anxious to see the photos, so get an estimate from your photographer and be sure to let them know when they should expect to receive the images!

8.   SHARE WITH VENDORS AND SUBMIT TO BLOGS

Once the photographer has finished editing the photos and you get that glorious notification in your inbox, share the love! Forward them to everyone who helped out; it will make their day! If you plan on submitting the photos to any blogs, research their submission requirements. You may need to have your photographer adjust the sizes of the images to ensure they fit the guidelines. Don't be discouraged if you get turned down by your favorite wedding blog. Just move on to the next one and try again! If your styled shoot ends up getting published, that's amazing! If it doesn't, you'll still have some incredible images to show off your talents to prospective clients. It's a win no matter what!

APPENDIX I

RANDOM BITS OF ADVICE

My number one piece of advice is (you've already heard this but it's worth mentioning again), don't assume anything! You need to *know* who is doing every single task. *Know* who is bringing what. *Know* what time each vendor is arriving. And (one more time for good measure), how do we *know* everything? We ask *all* the questions!

Be sure to ask hair stylists and makeup artists ahead of time what types of payments they can accept on the wedding day! Sometimes they will only accept cash and, unless this is known ahead of time, most people will only have their debit or credit cards on them.

If your client has planned for flowers to be added to the cake, make sure it is clear who will be putting them on. Sometimes the florist prefers to do this and other times the baker will insist on doing it. You definitely want to make sure somebody does it, so be sure to get this established before the wedding day! Also, make sure the deliveries are timed properly so that whoever *is* doing it has what they need when they need it!

For any rented items, make sure there is a clear plan for getting the items returned. And make sure your clients are fully aware of that plan! Will the rental company return to pick them up? If so, when? Will it be at the end of the night or the next day? Or will it be the next business day? If that's the case, make sure that doesn't conflict with any venue policies and that someone will be on-site to be sure the rental company staff are able to get in. If the clients are responsible for returning any items, be sure they know when the items are due back. Will it be the next day, the next business day, or within one week? This is especially important for clients who have travelled from out of state! If the wedding is on

Saturday and they are heading back home on Sunday, but the rentals can't be returned until Monday, that could be a problem!

If your clients are providing any signage (e.g. welcome sign, seating assignment board, quote board, bar menu, etc.) or large photo prints, make certain they are also providing easels or stands to hold them! It is surprisingly one of the most overlooked décor details.

Occasionally, clients who are looking for ways to cut back on some of their costs will come up with a plan to purchase their linens instead of renting them. Typically, this plan includes the idea that they will sell them afterwards and recoup some of their costs. While this may seem like a great money-saving idea, the amount of extra work and hassle this adds oftentimes greatly outweighs any potential savings. First, they must all be ironed ahead of time. And believe me, this is no easy feat! A floor-length linen fit for an eight-foot banquet table is enormous! With a standard iron and ironing board, it would easily take an hour to press it and you still wouldn't likely be able to get all of those deep-set wrinkles out. People often assume that since they come packaged so neatly that they can just keep them packaged until the day of the wedding and they will have crisp, clean, wrinkle-free linens, but that is so not the case! They actually look terrible fresh out of the package! Also, even if they were able to iron them all beforehand, there is still the matter of transporting them without re-wrinkling them. This would involve expertly folding them and draping them over hangers. Remember, these linens are huge and even folded, you'd still need a good amount of car space to keep them from wrinkling during travel. Again, not as easy as it sounds! In addition, they'd either have to set them on the tables themselves, or pay for extra staff to do it. And that's just the beginning! Afterwards they'll have to collect them all and transport them home (with some covered in food, wine, beer, etc.). They would need to be washed within 24 hours to avoid any molding, but properly shaken out first so they don't end up with bits of food in their washing machine! That's assuming their washing machine can handle linens of that size. Stains would need to be treated and if any candle wax happened to get on any, forget it! Things get even more complicated if it's a specialty linen. Have you ever seen frosting on a payette sequin linen? It's a mess! And, as you might have guessed, they are not so easy to sell. So, trust me when I say, it is so much better (for everyone involved) to just rent the linens and let the experts handle it!

Speaking of linens, be sure your clients have thought through their linen sizes. Do they want their linens to drape all the way to the floor or just halfway down? Are they using any toppers or runners? Be sure they have planned for the correct sizes for their intended look. Also, be sure they haven't forgotten about any specialty tables (e.g. gift table, guestbook table, dessert table, and DJ table, if applicable).

And since we're on the topic of tables, make sure you know who is providing what and who needs what! Does the caterer need tables (and linens) provided for the buffet, appetizer table, or beverage station? Does the DJ provide his own table or does he need one? How about a chair? Does the band need any tables or chairs? These things are easy to assume, but easier to assume incorrectly, so make sure you *know*!

If your client's wedding day plans involve setting up a tent, you may have some additional measures to take in order to ensure it complies with local laws or ordinances. Some municipalities require the incorporation of a long list of fire safety measures (such as illuminated exit signs and fire extinguishers) into the utilization of any tents. It will often depend on the property upon which the tent will be constructed, whether it is public or private. It's also a good idea (and perhaps even a requirement) to have the ground screened for any public utility lines before having the tent placed. Setting up these big tents involves driving large stakes into the ground and if one of those stakes punctures a utility line, you'll have a very big problem on your hands! Check with the local governing entity to see if there are any special requirements or considerations regarding the construction of a tent.

Pay special attention to the timing of deliveries, setup plans, and vendor arrival times. For example, you don't want the florist hauling in twenty centerpieces only to find all of the tables still awaiting linens! You want to be sure everything is planned out in sequence so that everyone can make the best use of their time. Some vendors will have other deliveries to make afterwards so if they're not able to complete their setup at the designated time, you may be stuck doing it yourself!

Make sure your clients have made plans for lunch! Sometimes this important part of the day gets overlooked and, depending on the location of the venue, there may not be many options for someone to easily run out and grab some food. Have them delegate this task to a wedding party member or a parent. You don't want a "hangry" bride!

Ask the DJ (or whoever is handling the sound for the ceremony) what type of microphone they will be providing. Some clients have strong feelings about not having a mic stand in their wedding pictures. If it's a handheld microphone, be sure that works for the officiant. It may be difficult to hold if they are also going to be holding a binder or book at the same time. You might need to add a table or stand to the altar if one is not already being provided. If it will be a lapel mic, ask the sound person if they believe the lapel mic will pick up the bride's and groom's voices as well, or if an additional microphone will be needed for them. If there are any readers or other participants with a speaking role, consider what they will use. Sometimes the sound person will provide an extra handheld microphone to be used in this scenario.

Be sure your clients have included their vendors in their meal counts! Some vendors will specify this in their contract, others won't, but it's customary to provide vendors with a meal. Don't worry about the catering staff, of course, they will take care of themselves. It's considerate to reach out to each vendor to discuss any dietary restrictions or food allergies. Also, don't forget about any assistants that will be accompanying any of the vendors! They'll need to eat too! Sometimes caterers will give their clients the option to select boxed lunches for their vendors. While most vendors won't mind, be aware that some vendors will have it listed in their contract that they require a hot meal. Also, be sure there will be a place for the vendors to sit for dinner. It can be an extra guest table or a table and chairs thrown together in a separate room, just as long as there is enough space for each vendor.

Pay close attention to the photographer's hours of service. This is another one of those areas that clients often don't give enough thought to. If your client is expecting to get some getting ready photos *and* photos of the sparkler exit at the end of the night, make sure their photographer's hours of service will cover this span of time. A six-hour shooting time, for example, will not likely be sufficient for your client's needs. Also, be sure to get a clear arrival and departure time from the photographer to help ensure your client's desired photos can be captured within that timeframe.

If your clients plan on doing family photos after the ceremony, ask them to put together an organized list of each group shot they want. In most cases, the photographer will ask for this as well. If they already have one completed, request a copy. Ask your clients to touch base with anyone on the list to let them know ahead of time that they will be needed for photos after the ceremony. Also, ask your client to designate at least one person who is familiar with the family to help coordinate the groups during the photos. This will help streamline the process and avoid any unnecessary delays.

Be sure to determine who will be cutting the cake! More often than not, the caterers will offer this as an add-on service to their contract, but it can't be assumed. I have come across caterers who refuse to touch any food they did not provide. Even if they do offer the service, they will still need to know in advance to plan (and bill) accordingly. What will the caterers do with the cake after they slice it? Will it be served to the guests or plated and set out on a dessert table? If it will be self-serve, be sure there is enough space on the dessert table to set out all those slices of cake!

Sometimes couples choose to freeze the top tier of their cake (or a cupcake or slice of pie) to share on their first anniversary. Check with your clients to see if this is something they would like to do. If so, be sure to make the caterers aware of their plan as well. Also, when the desserts get delivered, be sure to ask the baker to leave one or two boxes behind. The clients will need something to take any leftovers or saved pieces home in!

If your clients aren't planning on providing coffee at the reception, ask them to reconsider! Inevitably, some guests will be downright perturbed if there is no coffee served at the reception. And they'll let you know about it! Encourage your clients to ensure that coffee will be available to their guests at some point during the reception. Typically, coffee is expected to be available after dinner or with dessert. Many of your clients will just assume that this is something the caterer automatically provides, but that's not usually the case. If you don't see it on the contract, it's probably not included. If your clients do decide to add coffee service to the catering contract, be sure that they will also be providing coffee mugs and coffee accessories (like cream, sugar, and stir sticks). Also, make sure it's clear whether the coffee will be served by the catering staff or setup at a self-serve beverage station. If it's the latter, you'll need to figure out where the coffee station will be placed and if an additional table and linen will need to be provided for this.

If your client has opted for dinner to be served family style, be sure to remind them to keep the table décor minimal. A lush floral arrangement and a ring of votives might not be the best option in this case. If your clients refuse to budge on their décor, have them connect with their caterer to discuss some alternative options. I've seen caterers remove centerpieces ahead of dinner and replace them afterwards to accommodate their client's family style request (although you can almost certainly count on an extra fee for that service)!

If your clients have chosen a buffet style dinner, ask the caterers if the guests will access the buffet from one side of the buffet table or both sides. This factor greatly impacts the amount of time dinner service will take. A one-sided buffet can take a large group a very long time to get through. If possible, request that both sides of the buffet be open to guests.

While most caterers will provide their own dinnerware, some will require that the client rents all plates, glassware, flatware, and serving dishes from a separate rental company. Occasionally, a client will *opt* to rent custom dinnerware (like vintage china) instead of using the standard dinnerware provided by their caterer, in order to achieve their desired look. Whatever the reason, if your client is renting dinnerware outside of the contract with their caterer, there will be some additional things to consider. Be sure to request a detailed list of items that will be needed, along with estimated amounts for each item, from the catering manager. If left up to the clients to figure out on their own, they may overlook things like bread baskets, butter knives, condiment dishes, extra linen napkins, or tongs for the salad. The caterer should review the rental list to ensure nothing has been forgotten. Be sure the client includes a few extras of each item, particularly flatware and napkins, because, as you know, stuff happens! People show up unexpectedly or things get dropped. Make sure dessert plates and forks (or bowls and spoons for ice cream) have been included. Additionally, if the clients are having a dessert buffet where several different dessert options will be available, it's a good idea to double the amount of dessert plates!

When dishes are rented, who is responsible for them becomes a bit of a grey area. First, you need to know in what condition the rental company requires them to be in upon their return (rinsed, hand-washed, or just scraped off). They will likely need to be repackaged in the same containers and manner in which they were delivered. Second, it is important that you very clearly determine who will be responsible for this. Again, while most caterers include this in their service (possibly for an added fee), there are some caterers out there who simply won't touch dishes that aren't their own. If that's the case, you'll need to bring some extra hands on board! You can either have your clients directly hire some additional helpers through a staffing agency, or you can take it upon yourself to do the hiring. If you opt for the latter, you'll need to collect the staffing agency's fee from your clients along with an additional fee to cover the extra work you are putting in by taking on this added responsibility. These same considerations need to be made with bartenders when your clients are required to rent the glassware from a separate company.

Another case of "whose job is it" comes up when your clients hire a food truck to provide a late-night snack to their guests. These mini-meals are typically served in or on disposable dishes, but that doesn't mean that the guests will be the ones disposing of them! Most of the time these get left on tables, or sometimes even littered around the property. Your clients may need to consider hiring a cleanup crew or perhaps you could arrange to provide a helper for an added fee.

If your clients are planning on doing a sparkler send-off, make sure they get the longer sparklers! The standard six-inch sparklers are way too short and you'll likely still be lighting guests' sparklers further down the line when the first ones begin to burn out. It kind of ruins the whole look! The eighteen to twenty-inch sparklers work great! The best way to prep for this is to bring a metal bucket prefilled with sand or dirt. Before getting the guests lined up, open up all of the sparkler boxes and place the sparklers (stick end down) into the sand-filled bucket. This way, you won't have twenty people trying to grab one out of your hand all at once. You'll know what I mean soon enough! Recruit three or four guests to assist you with lighting the sparklers. I always make sure to bring at least four long lighters for this exact reason! Get the guests lined up in two rows.

Starting from the front, ask the first four people down the line to put the tips of their sparklers together. This will allow you to light four sparklers at a time! Proceed down the rest of the line in the same manner. They take a minute to catch so be patient. Instruct your helpers to do this as well. You can have two of you start at the front of the lines and the other two can start halfway down the lines. This will help to ensure the sparklers get lit as quickly as possible without too many burning out before you're ready! While the couple is walking through the sparkler aisle, see if you can find a place to dump the sand. Once the sparkler send-off is finished, have the guests drop their used sparkler sticks into the bucket for easy disposal. It certainly beats rummaging around in the dark picking sharp metal sticks up off the ground!

Occasionally vendors will need a signature from someone confirming that they have done their job. They'll usually come to you for this signature, but I would advise against signing any documents on behalf of your clients. Discuss this with your clients ahead of time and have *them* decide who you should seek out if and when a signature is needed. When they know to expect this, it won't seem like such an inconvenience when it happens.

ABOUT THE AUTHOR

Allison is a party planner turned wedding coordinator with over six years of experience helping couples enjoy a stress-free wedding day! Her wedding designs have been featured in Bespoke Bride, The Pretty Blog, and Wedding Day Magazine. She was awarded Thumbtack's "best of" for four consecutive years and is the recipient of Wedding Wire's Couples' Choice Award.

Made in the USA
Columbia, SC
14 July 2024

38609868R00095